PHILIPPIANS, COLOSSIANS and PHILEMON

William MacDonald

LUKE 24:27

Original text material by William MacDonald
Developed as a correspondence course by
Emmaus Correspondence School,
Which is an extension ministry of
Emmaus Bible College
founded in 1941.

The author acknowledges the assistance of Dr. R. E. Harlow and Mr. Kevin Dyer, both of whom read the notes on Philippians in manuscript form and offered helpful comments and constructive criticisms.

The author also expresses sincere thanks for the help received from Messrs. Cecil Greenhow, Walter Munro, and George D. Lyon; they read the manuscript of the notes on Colossians and offered many helpful suggestions.

A special acknowledgment is due to Mr. Robert Little for his thorough editing of the notes on Colossians. He reviewed the preliminary manuscript; then he went over the corrected version, submitting seven typewritten pages of suggested additions and corrections.

The author wishes to thank the Macmillan Company for permission to quote from Phillips' NEW TESTAMENT IN MODERN ENGLISH, 1958.

ISBN 0-940293-40-4

89/987654

Instructions to Students

This correspondence course is a verse-by-verse study of Paul's letters to the saints at Philippi and to the saints at Colosse and also of his brief note to Philemon. It seeks to explain the general meaning of each of the letters in a simple and understandable manner.

However, no commentary can ever take the place of the Word itself. The best it can hope to do is to give the general flow of thought, then send the student back to the Bible to search for the precious truths that lie in it.

If this course is used as an end in itself, it becomes a snare rather than a help; if it is used to stimulate personal study of the sacred Scriptures, then it will achieve its goal.

The Bible is inexhaustible, and no commentator could ever give the full meaning of even a single verse.

Not only so, but the Bible is authoritative. We are to be guided by what the Bible says, and not by what men say. Thus, the student should test all teaching by the Word of God, and hold fast to that which is good.

HOW TO STUDY

In order to derive the greatest benefit from the course, always have your Bible opened to the passage being studied. First read a verse in the Bible, then make a mental note of any questions you might have on the meaning of that verse. It is especially helpful to try to express the meaning in your own words. After making this personal attempt to grasp the apostle's thought, read the comments in this course.

Chapters and verses being discussed are indicated in the margin of the text throughout the course.

HOW THIS COURSE IS ORGANIZED

PHILIPPIANS
1. The Joyful Prisoner (1:1-30)
2. Sacrifice and Service (2:1-30)
3. Pitfalls Along the Way (3:1-21)
4. Victorious Living (4:1-23)

COLOSSIANS
5. For You I Am Praying (1:1-14)
6. The Glories of Christ (1:15-23)
7. The Ministry and the Mystery (1:24—2:7)
8. Spiritual Perils (2:8-23)
9. New Lives for Old (3:1-17)
10. Concluding Advice and Greetings (3:18—4:18)

PHILEMON
11. Praise for Philemon (1-7)
12. The Plea for Onesimus (8-25)

BIBLIOGRAPHY

EXAMS

Each exam covers two lessons. (Exam 1, for example, covers lessons 1 and 2.) Each exam is clearly marked to show you which questions deal with which lesson. You may take the exam in two stages. When you have completed lesson 1, you may take the part of Exam 1 dealing with that lesson.

You may use any version of the Bible for general study. When answering exam questions, however, restrict yourself to either the *Authorized (King James) Version* (1611), or the *American Standard Version* (1901). These are two widely used versions. There are so many versions today that your instructor cannot possibly check them all in evaluating your work.

1. Thought and Research Questions

Some exams contain questions designed to make you do original Bible study. You may use your Bible to answer these questions. They are clearly marked.

2. What Do You Say? Questions

Questions headed in this way are optional and no point value is assigned to them. You may freely state your own opinions in answer to such questions. Your candid answers will help your instructor get to know you better as an individual. They will also help us evaluate the general effectiveness of this course.

3. How Your Papers Are Graded

Any incorrectly answered questions will be marked by your instructor. You will be referred back to the place in the Bible or the textbook where the correct answer is to be found.

GROUP ENROLLMENTS

If you are enrolled in a class, submit your exam papers to the leader or secretary of the class who will send them for the entire group to the Correspondence School.

GENERAL INSTRUCTIONS

Begin studying immediately, or if you are in a group, as soon as the group beings. Try to keep a regular schedule. You will be allowed a maximum of one year to complete this course from the time of enrollment. Many students endeavor to complete at least one lesson each week, submitting exams every two weeks. We highly recommend the adoption of some such study schedule.

Lesson One

The Joyful Prisoner

Philippians 1:1-30

I. Salutation (vv. 1, 2).
II. Paul's praise for the saints (vv. 3-8).
III. Paul's prayer for the saints (vv. 9-11).
IV. Paul's imprisonment promotes the gospel (vv. 12-18).
V. Paul's prospects (vv. 19-26).
VI. Paul's plea for perseverance and patience (vv. 27-30).

INTRODUCTION

It was a momentous day in the history of Christian missions. The apostle Paul had come as far as Troas on his second missionary journey. Troas was located on the northwest coast of Asia Minor, across the Aegean Sea from Greece. In a vision one night, a man of Macedonia appeared to the apostle, saying, "Come over into Macedonia, and help us" (Acts 16:9). Immediately the apostle Paul arranged to sail for Macedonia with Timothy, and also with Luke and Silas. They first set foot on European soil at Neapolis, then journeyed inland to Philippi. The latter city was at that time a Roman colony, governed by Roman officials, and granting the rights and privileges of Roman citizenship to its inhabitants.

On the sabbath day, the gospel preachers went down by a riverside where a group of women were in the habit of gathering for prayer (Acts

16:13). One of these was Lydia, a seller of purple, from the city of Thyatira in Asia Minor. When she accepted the gospel message, she became the first convert to Christianity on the continent of Europe.

But Paul's stay in Philippi did not prove entirely peaceful. A young woman possessed with a spirit of divination (foretelling future events) met the servants of the Lord and for some time followed them, crying out, "These men are the servants of the most high God, which shew unto us the way of salvation" (Acts 16:17). Not willing to accept the testimony of one possessed by an evil spirit, the apostle Paul commanded the demon to come out of her. When her masters, who had profited from this girl's predictions, saw what had happened, they were furious with the apostle Paul. They dragged him and Silas into the market place before the representatives of Rome. These magistrates, in turn, commanded that they should be beaten and cast into prison.

The story of what happened in that prison at Philippi is now well-known. At midnight, Paul and Silas were praying and singing praises unto God. Suddenly there was a great earthquake, opening all the doors of the prison and causing the bands of the prisoners to be loosed. The jailor, thinking that the prisoners had escaped, was about to kill himself when Paul reassured him that his inmates had not fled. It was then that the jailor cried out, "Sirs, what must I do to be saved?" The memorable answer came back, "Believe on the Lord Jesus Christ and thou shalt be saved" (Acts 16:31). God's grace had won another trophy at Philippi. In the morning, the local authorities urged Paul and his companions to leave town as quickly as possible. This Paul refused to do. He reminded them that they had beaten him, a Roman citizen, and had imprisoned him without a fair trial. After continued appeals from the magistrates to leave the city, Paul and his companions first went to visit in the home of Lydia and then took their leave (Acts 16:40).

It was about ten years after this that Paul wrote his letter to the Philippians. He was again imprisoned. The exact location is not definitely known. It is commonly supposed that the epistle was written in Rome, although it might also have been in Caesarea, Ephesus, or Corinth. The Philippians had heard that Paul was in prison, so they sent a gift of money to him. Epaphroditus had been commissioned to carry this gift to Paul. After delivering it, he decided to stay there awhile and help the apostle in his affliction. Epaphroditus himself took sick in carrying out these duties; in fact, he nearly died of sickness. But God had mercy on him and raised him back to health once again. He is now ready to go back to Philippi, to his home assembly, and so the apostle Paul is sending back this letter of acknowledgment with him.

The letter is one of the most personal and affectionate of Paul's epistles. It reveals clearly that this assembly held a very special place of esteem in his affection. As we read it, we detect the very tender bond that existed between the great apostle Paul and this church which he had founded.

SALUTATION (1:1-2)

Paul and Timothy are linked together at the opening of this letter. This **1:1** does not mean that Timothy helped to write the epistle. He had been with Paul when he first visited Philippi; therefore, he was known to the saints there. Now Timothy is with Paul as the apostle pens this letter. Paul was now an older man (Philemon 9), while Timothy was still quite young. Thus were age and youth yoked together in the service of the best of Masters. "It is the union of springtime and autumn; of enthusiasm and experience; of impulse and wisdom; of tender hope and quiet and rich assurance"—Jowett. Both are described as servants of Christ Jesus. Both loved their Master. The ties of Calvary bound them to the service of their Savior forever.

The letter is addressed to all the saints in Christ Jesus at Philippi, with the bishops and deacons. We shall find that the word *all* recurs in this epistle quite frequently. Paul's affectionate interest went out to *all* the Lord's people. "The saints in Christ Jesus which are at Philippi" describes the dual position of the believers. As to their spiritual status, they were set apart by God in Christ Jesus. As to their geographical location, they were at Philippi. Two places at the same time! Then the apostle mentions the bishops and the deacons. The bishops were the elders or overseers in the assembly—those who took a pastoral interest in the flock of God and who led the flock by their godly example. The deacons, on the other hand, were the servants of the church who

3

were probably chiefly concerned with its material affairs, such as finances, etc.

There were only these three groups in the assembly—saints, bishops, and deacons. If there had been a clergyman in charge, Paul would have mentioned him also. Instead he speaks only of bishops (plural) and deacons (also plural). Here we have a remarkable picture of the simplicity of assembly life in the early days of the church age. The saints are mentioned first, then their spiritual guides, and then their temporal servants. That is all!

1:2   In Paul's characteristic greeting, he wishes the saints grace and peace. The former is not so much the grace which comes to a sinner at the time of his conversion as the grace which he must constantly obtain at the throne of grace to help in every time of need (Hebrews 4:16). Likewise, the peace which Paul craves for them is not so much peace with God, which is theirs already, as the peace of God which comes through prayer and thanksgiving (4:6). Both of these blessings come from God our Father and the Lord Jesus Christ! Notice how the apostle honors the Son even as he honors the Father (John 5:23). There is no mistaking that, to him, Jesus Christ is God.

PRAISE FOR THE SAINTS (1:3-8)

1:3 Now Paul bursts into a song of thanksgiving. But that is nothing new for the apostle. The walls of the Philippian jail had echoed the songs of Paul and Silas on their first visit there. As he writes, he is probably a prisoner in Rome—but he is still singing "songs in the night." The indomitable Paul! Every remembrance of the Philippians awakened thanksgiving in his heart. Not only were they his children in the faith, but in many ways they had proved to be a model church.

1:4   In every prayer, he made supplication for the Philippians with joy. To him, it was a sheer delight to pray for them—not dull drudgery. From this and from many similar passages in Paul's writing, we learn that he was a man of prayer. It is not necessary to search further for the reason why he was so wonderfully used of God. When we remember the extent of his travels and the host of Christians he knew, we marvel

4

that he maintained such a personal, intimate interest in them all.

The specific reason for Paul's thanksgiving was their fellowship in **1:5** furtherance of the gospel "from the first day until now." "Fellowship" here might include financial assistance, but it extends also to prayer support and a wholehearted devotion to the spread of the good news.

When Paul mentions "the first day," one cannot help wondering if the jailor was still alive when this letter was publicly read to the assembly at Philippi. If so, this mention of Paul's introduction to the Philippians would certainly have struck a responsive chord in his heart.

As the apostle thinks of the good start the believers have made in **1:6** the Christian life, he is assured that God will finish the good work He has begun.

> "The work which His grace has begun,
> The arm of His strength will complete."

The "good work" here may refer to their salvation, or it may mean their active participation in the furtherance of the gospel. "The day of Jesus Christ" refers to the time of His coming again to take His people home to heaven and probably also includes the judgment seat of Christ, when service for Him will be reviewed and rewarded.

Paul feels justified in being thus thankful for the Philippians. In **1:7** his heart he treasures a lasting memory of how loyally they stood with him, whether he was in prison, or travelling about "in the defence and confirmation of the gospel." Moffatt translates this verse helpfully, as follows: "It is only natural for me to be thinking of you all in this way, for alike in my prison and as I defend and vindicate the gospel, I bear in mind how you all share with me in the grace divine."

"The defence of the gospel" refers to the ministry of answering the critics, while "the confirmation of the gospel" relates rather to establishing the message more firmly in the hearts of those who are already believers. "The gospel both overthrows its foes and strengthens its friends"—Vine.

The expression "ye are all partakers of my grace" is more correctly translated "ye all are partakers with me of grace." Grace here means the undeserved strength from God to carry on the work of the Lord in the face of severe opposition.

The memory of their faithful cooperation makes the apostle **1:8**

5

long to be with them again. He calls God to witness how greatly he yearns for them "in the bowels of Jesus Christ." In those days, the bowels were considered to be the seat of the affections. Today we would say how greatly I long for you "with tender Christian affection" —Weymouth. Paul's expression of love is all the more remarkable when we remember that he had been born a Jew and that he was writing to people of Gentile descent. The grace of God had broken down the ancient hatred, and now they were all one in Christ Jesus.

PRAYER FOR THE SAINTS (1:9-11)

1:9 Thanksgiving now gives way to prayer. Will Paul ask for them wealth, or comfort, or freedom from trouble? No, he asks that their love might constantly increase in knowledge and discernment. At first, this is a rather difficult thought to understand. Just what does it mean? First of all, we should understand that the primary aim of the Christian life is to love God and to love one's fellow man. But love is not just a matter of the emotions. In effective service for the Lord, we must use our intelligence and exercise discernment. Otherwise our efforts are apt to be futile. So Paul is here praying not only that the Philippians will continue in the display of Christian love, but also that their love will be exercised in full knowledge and discernment.

1:10 Love that is thus enlightened will enable them to discern the things that are more excellent. In all realms of life, some things are good and others are better. The good is oftentimes the enemy of the best. For effective service, these distinctions must be made. Love that is enlightened will also enable them to avoid what is questionable or downright wrong. Paul would have them sincere, that is, utterly transparent, and blameless in view of the day of Christ. To be blameless does not mean to be sinless. We all commit sins, but the blameless person is the one who confesses and forsakes the sin, asking forgiveness from those who were wronged and making restitution whenever possible. "The day of Christ" in this verse is probably the same as "the day of Jesus Christ" in verse 6. It refers to the rapture and to the judgment of the believer's works that follow.

6

The final petition of the apostle's prayer is that the Christians 1:11 might be filled with the fruit of righteousness, that is, with the fruit which righteousness produces, or with all the Christian virtues that make up a righteous life. The source of these virtues is Jesus Christ, and their object is the glory and praise of God.

"Bearing the while a full harvest of righteousness, attained through Jesus our Messiah, and redounding to the praise and glory of God"—Way. Guy King points out that this petition of Paul is exactly parallel to the words in Isaiah 61:3, "that they might be called trees of righteousness (being filled with the fruits of righteousness), the planting of the Lord (which are by Jesus Christ), that he might be glorified (unto the glory and praise of God)."

"The word 'fruit' . . . is associated closely with our relation to Christ and His expectation of us. The branches on a vine are intended to bear fruit"—Lehman Strauss.

PAUL'S IMPRISONMENT PROMOTES THE GOSPEL (1:12-18)

The prayer is ended. Paul next rehearses his blessings, that is, the bene- 1:12 fits that have resulted from his imprisonment. Jowett calls this section "The Fortune of Misfortune."

The apostle would have the brethren know that the things that happened to him, that is, his trial and imprisonment, have resulted in the furtherance of the gospel rather than in its hindrance, as might have been expected. This is another wonderful illustration of how God overrules the wicked plans of demons and of men and brings triumph out of seeming tragedy and beauty from ashes. "Man has his wickedness, but God has His way."

The apostle explains that, first of all, his bonds have become man- 1:13 ifest as being in Christ. By this he means that it has become widely known that he was imprisoned as a result of his testimony for the Lord Jesus Christ and not as a criminal or an evildoer. The expression "my bonds in Christ" really means "my imprisonment as being for the sake of Christ."

The real reason for his bonds became well-known throughout the palace and in all other places. The word translated "palace" may mean (1) the whole praetorian guard, that is, the Roman soldiers who guarded the palace where the emperor dwelt, or (2) the whole praetorium itself. The praetorium was the palace and here would include all of its occupants. In any event, Paul is saying that his imprisonment has served as a testimony to the representatives of the Roman imperial power where he was. "The very chain which Roman discipline riveted on the prisoner's arm secured to his side a hearer who would tell the story of patient suffering for Christ, among those who, the next day, might be in attendance on Nero himself"—T. W. Drury.

1:14   A second favorable outcome of his imprisonment was that other Christians were thereby encouraged to be more fearless in testifying for the Lord Jesus. Persecution often has the effect of transforming quiet and bashful believers into courageous witnesses.

1:15   The motive in some hearts was jealousy and rivalry. We would say today that they preached Christ out of envy and contentiousness. Others had sincere and pure motives; they preached Christ out of good **1:16** will, in an honest effort to help the apostle. The envious preachers wanted to make Paul's imprisonment more bitter. Their message was good, but their temper was bad. "The nature of religious activity is such that much of it can be carried on for reasons that are not good, such as anger, jealousy, ambition, vanity and avarice"—Tozer. This teaches the necessity for watching our motives when we serve the Lord Christ. We must not do it for self-display, for the advancement of a religious sect, or for the defeat of other Christians. Here, incidentally, is a good example of the necessity for our love to be exercised in knowledge and discernment, as we saw in verse 9.

1:17   Others were preaching the gospel with pure and sincere love, knowing that Paul was determined to defend the gospel. There was nothing selfish or sectarian or cruel in their service. They knew very well that Paul had been committed to prison because of his bold stand for the gospel. So they determined to carry on the work while he was **1:18** thus confined. Paul refuses to be downcast by the wrong motives of some. Christ is being preached by both groups, and that is, for him, great cause for rejoicing. "Think of him in prison . . . debarred from the work that he loved, and others taking advantage of his absence to grieve

8

him, preaching the very gospel out of contention and strife, and yet his heart was so running over with joy, that he was filling others with it" —William Kelly.

PAUL'S PROSPECTS (1:19-26)

The outlook is encouraging. The apostle knows that the whole course 1:19 of events will lead to his salvation. The word "salvation" is used in several different ways in the New Testament. First of all, it refers to the eternal deliverance from the penalty of sin which a sinner receives when he trusts the Lord Jesus Christ. Then it also refers to day by day deliverance from the power of sin in a believer's life. Again, it describes the believer's future deliverance from the presence of sin when he is taken home to heaven. A fourth use of the word is to describe deliverance from physical danger, personal injury, sickness, or imprisonment. It is this last meaning that is found in verse 19. Salvation here does not mean the salvation of Paul's soul, but rather his liberation from prison. The means which God will use in effecting his release will be the prayers of the Philippians and the ministry or help of the Spirit of Jesus Christ. Marvel here at the importance which Paul puts upon the prayers of a feeble band of believers. He sees them as sufficiently powerful to thwart the purposes and the mighty power of Rome.

The supply of the Spirit of Jesus Christ means the power of the Holy Spirit stretched forth in his behalf—the strength which the Spirit would supply to him. In general, it refers to "the boundless resources which the Spirit supplies to enable believers to stand fast, regardless of what the circumstances may be."

As he thought of the prayers of the Christians and the assistance 1:20 of the Holy Spirit, Paul expressed his eager desire and hope that he might never be ashamed, but rather that he might always have a fearless and outspoken witness for Christ. And no matter what the outcome of judicial processes might be—whether he was to be freed or put to death —his ambition was that Christ should be magnified in his body. To magnify does not mean to make Christ greater. He is already great, and nothing we can do will make Him greater. But to magnify means to

9

cause Christ to be esteemed or praised by others.

Christ can be magnified by our bodies in life—"magnified by lips that bear happy testimony to Him; magnified by hands employed in His happy service; magnified by feet only too happy to go on His errands; magnified by knees happily bent in prayer for His kingdom; magnified by shoulders happy to bear one another's burdens"—Guy King. And Christ can be magnified by our bodies in death—bodies that have been worn out in His service; bodies that have been pierced by savage spears; bodies that have been torn by stones or burned at the stake.

1:21   Here, in verse 21, is Paul's philosophy of life. He did not live for money, or fame, or pleasure. The object of his life was to love, worship, and serve the Lord Jesus. He wanted his life to be like the life of Christ. He wanted the Savior to live out His life through him. "And to die is gain." To die is to be with Christ and to be like Him forever. It is to serve Him with unsinning heart and with feet that never shall stray. We do not ordinarily think of death as one of our gains. Sad to say, the outlook today seems to be that "to live is earthly gain, and to die would be the end of gain." "To the Apostle Paul death was not a darksome passageway, where all our treasures rot away in a swift corruption; it was a place of gracious transition, 'a covered way that leadeth into light' "—Jowett.

1:22   Verse 22 is rather difficult to understand in the King James Version. What it probably means is this: If it is God's will for Paul to live a while longer in the flesh, then that will mean fruitful labor for him. He will be able to give further help to the Lord's people. But it was a difficult decision for him—whether to go to the Savior Whom he loved, or to remain on earth in the Lord's service, to which he was also very attached. He did not know which to choose.

1:23   To be "in a strait betwixt two" means to be required to make a difficult decision between two possibilities—that of going home to heaven or that of remaining on earth as an apostle of Christ Jesus. He ardently longed to depart to be with Christ, which is far better. If he only considered his own interests, this is doubtless the choice he would make.

Notice that Paul did not believe in any theory of soul-sleep. He believed that the Christian goes to be with Christ at the time of death

10

and that he is in the conscious enjoyment of the presence of the Lord. How ridiculous it would be for him to say, as some do today, in effect: "To live is Christ; to sleep is gain." Or, "To depart and to sleep is far better." "Sleep" is used in the New Testament of the believer's body at the time of death (1 Thessalonians 4:14), but never of his soul. Notice, too, that death is not to be confused with the coming of the Savior. At the time of death, we go to be with Him. At the time of the rapture, He comes to us.

For the sake of the Philippians, it was more necessary for Paul to   1:24
live on earth a while longer. One cannot but be impressed with the unselfishness of this great-hearted man. He does not think of his own comfort or ease, but rather of what will best advance the cause of Christ and the welfare of His people. Having this confidence—that he   1:25
was still needed on earth to instruct and comfort and encourage the saints—Paul knew that he would not be put to death at this time. How did he know? We believe that he lived so close to the Lord that the Holy Spirit was able to communicate this knowledge to him. "The secret of the Lord is with them that fear him" (Psalm 25:14). Those who dwell deep in God, in quiet meditation, hear secrets that are drowned out by the noise and rush and bustle of life today. "You have to be near to hear." Paul was near. By abiding in the flesh, Paul would be able to promote their spiritual progress and increase the joy that was theirs through trusting in the Lord.

Through his being spared for longer life and service on earth, the   1:26
Philippians would have added cause for rejoicing in the Lord when he would visit them once again. Can you not imagine how they would throw their arms around him and kiss him, and praise the Lord with deep rejoicing when he would arrive at Philippi? Perhaps they would say, "Well, Paul, we prayed for you, but honestly, we never expected to see you here again. But how we praise the Lord that He has given you back to us once more!"

PAUL'S PLEA (1:27-30)

Paul now adds a word of caution. "Only let your conversation be as it   1:27

11

becometh the gospel of Christ." Conversation here means not just one's speech, but one's whole manner of life or one's citizenship. Those who are Christians should be Christ-like. Citizens of heaven should behave accordingly. We should be in practice what we are in position. In addition to this plea for consistency, the apostle makes an appeal for constancy. Specifically, he desires that whether he comes to them personally, or, being absent, hears reports about them, he may know that they are standing fast with a common spirit, and unitedly laboring earnestly for the faith of the gospel, that is, the Christian faith. Christians face a common foe; they should not fight each other but should unite against the enemy.

1:28   Neither were they to be afraid of the enemies of the gospel. Fearlessness in the face of persecution has a twofold meaning. First, it is an omen of destruction to those who fight against God. Secondly, it is a sign of salvation to those who brave the wrath of the foe. "Salvation" is here probably used in its future tense, referring to the eventual deliverance of the saint from trial and the redemption of his body as well as his spirit and soul. "Your fearlessness will be to them a sure token of impending destruction, but to you it will be a sure token of your salvation"—Weymouth.

1:29   The Philippians should remember that it is a privilege to suffer for Christ as well as to believe on Him. Dr. Griffith John wrote that once when he was surrounded by a hostile Chinese crowd, and was beaten, he put his hand to his face and when he withdrew it, saw that it was bathed in blood. "He was possessed by an extraordinary sense of exaltation, and he rejoiced that he had been counted worthy to suffer for His Name." Is it not remarkable that even suffering is exalted by Christianity to such a lofty plane? Truly, even "an apparent trifle burns with the fire immortal when it is in communion with the Infinite." The cross dignifies and ennobles.

1:30   The connection of this verse with the previous one is better understood if we supply the words, "Since you are engaged in . . ." Thus it would read, "The privilege of suffering for Christ has been granted to you, since you are engaged in the same kind of conflict which you saw in me when I was in Philippi and which you now hear that I am still waging."

When you have mastered this lesson, take the first part of Exam 1 (covering lesson 1), questions 1-10 on pages **29-30**.

Lesson Two

Sacrifice and Service

Philippians 2:1-30

I. Exhortation to unity and to consideration for others (vv. 1-4).
II. The Lord Jesus as an Example of humility and sacrifice (vv. 5-11).
III. Exhortation to work out their salvation by the strength divine (vv. 12, 13).
IV. Warning against complaints and disputes (v. 14).
V. Exhortation to behave as:
   a. Sons of God (v. 15).
   b. Light-bearers (v. 15).
   c. Proclaimers of the Word of Life (v. 16).
VI. Paul's example of sacrifice (vv. 17, 18).
VII. Timothy's example of unselfish service (vv. 19-24).
VIII. Epaphroditus' example of living for others (vv. 25-30).

CONSIDERATION OF OTHERS (2:1-4)

Although the assembly at Philippi was exemplary in many respects, and Paul had occasion to commend the saints warmly, yet there was an undercurrent of strife. We know, for instance, that there was a difference of opinion between two women, Euodias and Syntyche (4:2). It is helpful to keep this in mind as we study chapter 2 because here the apostle is dealing directly with the cause and cure of contentions among the people of God.   **2:1**

15

The student should understand, first of all, that the "if" in this verse is not the "if" of doubt but of argument. The verse lists four great considerations which should draw believers together in harmony and cooperation. The apostle is saying, in effect: "*Since* there is so much of encouragement in Christ, *since* His love has such a tremendous persuasiveness, *since* the Holy Spirit brings us all together in such a wonderful fellowship, and *since* there is so much of tender mercies and compassions in Christianity, we should all be able to get along in happy harmony with one another." F. B. Meyer describes these four motives as (1) the persuasiveness of Christ; (2) the tender care that love gives; (3) the sharing of the Spirit; (4) humaneness and pity. At any rate, it is clear that the apostle Paul is making an appeal for unity based upon common devotion to Christ and common possession of the Holy Spirit. "With all that there is in Christ, the members of His body should have unity of purpose, affection, accord, sympathy."

2:2   If these foregoing arguments carry any weight with the Philippians, then Paul beseeches them, on the basis of such arguments, that they should make full his joy. Up to this time, the Philippians had indeed given Paul much joy. He does not deny that for a moment, but now he asks that they should fill the cup of his joy to overflowing. They could do this by being of the same mind, having the same love, and being of one accord and of one mind.

Does this mean that all Christians are expected to think alike and to act alike? The Word of God nowhere gives such a suggestion. While we are definitely expected to be agreed on the great fundamentals of the Christian faith, yet it is obvious that on many minor matters there will be a great deal of difference of opinion. Uniformity and unity are not the same thing. It is possible to have the latter without the former. Although we might not agree on minor matters, yet we can submerge our own opinions, where no real principle is involved, for the good of others.

"To be of the same mind" really means to have the mind of Christ, to see things as He would see them, and to respond as He would respond. "To have the same love" means to show the same love to others that the Lord has shown to us, a love that did not count the cost. "To be of one accord" means to work together in harmony toward a common goal. Finally, "to be of one mind" means to act so unitedly as to show that one Mind is directing our activities, namely, the Mind of the Lord Jesus.

Nothing should be done through strife or vainglory, since these are 2:3 two of the greatest enemies of unity among the people of God. Strife here really refers to party spirit or faction. Vainglory, on the other hand, speaks of pride or self-display. Wherever you find people who are interested in gathering a clique around themselves or in promoting their own interests, there you will find the seeds of contention and strife. The remedy is found in the latter part of the verse. "In lowliness of mind let each esteem other better than themselves." It is easy to read an exhortation like this in the Word of God, but it is quite another thing to appreciate what it really means, and then to put it into actual practice. To esteem others better than ourselves is utterly foreign to the human mind, and man cannot do it in his own strength. It is only as one is indwelt and empowered by the Holy Spirit that it can ever be practiced.

The cure of troubles among the people of God is to be more con- 2:4 cerned with the things of others than with the things of our own lives. In a very real way the word "others" forms the key of this chapter. It is as we give our lives in devoted service for others that we rise above the selfish strife of men.

> "Lord, help me live from day to day
> In such a self-forgetful way
> That even when I kneel to pray,
> My prayer shall be for—OTHERS.

> "Help me in all the work I do
> To ever be sincere and true
> And know that all I'd do for you,
> Must needs be done for—OTHERS.

> "Let 'Self' be crucified and slain
> And buried deep: and all in vain
> May efforts be to rise again,
> Unless to live for—OTHERS.

"And when my work on earth is done
And my new work in heaven's begun
May I forget the crown I've won,
While thinking still of—OTHERS.

"Others, Lord, yes, others,
Let this my motto be
Help me to live for others,
That I might live like Thee."
—C. D. Meigs

THE LORD'S SUPREME EXAMPLE (2:5-11)

2:5 Paul is now going to hold up before the eyes of the Philippians the example of the Lord Jesus Christ. What kind of an attitude did He exhibit? What characterized His behavior toward others? Guy King has well described the mind of the Lord Jesus as (1) the selfless mind; (2) the sacrificial mind; (3) the serving mind. The Lord Jesus consistently thought of others.

"He had no tears for His own griefs,
But sweat-drops of blood for mine."

2:6 When we read that Christ Jesus was in the form of God, we learn that He existed from all eternity as God. It does not mean that He merely resembled God, but that He actually is God in the truest sense of the word. He "thought it not robbery to be equal with God." This may have at least two possible meanings: (1) As stated in the King James Version, it may mean that He did not think it was at all improper for Him to be equal with God. It did not represent any seizing of honor or glory that was not His due. (2) The American Standard Version gives what we believe to be a truer meaning. He "counted not the being on an equality with God a thing to be grasped." Now as we have pointed out, the Lord Jesus was truly God, and from all eternity He was equal with God the Father. He dwelt in undisturbed bliss and glory in heaven.

18

He was not only equal with God as to His Person but also as to His circumstances. He enjoyed the same freedom from anything discordant or unpleasant.

But the Lord Jesus saw man's need for redemption. Seeing this, He did not feel that He must grasp the comforts and glories of heaven as a prize to be held at all cost. He "counted not the being on an equality with God a thing to be grasped." Thus He was willing to come into this world to endure the contradiction of sinners against Himself. God the Father was never spit upon or beaten or crucified. In this sense, the Father was greater than the Son—not greater as to His Person, but rather as to the manner in which He lived. The Lord Jesus expressed this thought in John 14:28: "If ye loved me, ye would rejoice, because I said, I go unto the Father; for my Father is greater than I." In other words, the disciples should have rejoiced to learn that He was going home to heaven. While here on earth, He had been cruelly treated and rejected. He had been in lower circumstances than His Father. In that sense, His Father was greater than He. But when He went back to heaven, He would be equal with the Father in *His circumstances* as well as in *His Person*.

"Thus it is not the nature or essence . . . but the mode of existence that is described in this clause, 'thought it not robbery to be equal with God'; and one mode of existence may be changed for another, though the essential nature is immutable. For example, St. Paul's own illustration in 2 Corinthians 8:9: 'Though He was rich, yet for your sakes He became poor, that ye through His poverty might be rich.' Here, in each case, there is a change of the mode of existence, but not of the nature. When a poor man becomes rich, his mode of existence is changed, but not his nature as man. It is so with the Son of God; from the rich and glorious mode of existence, which was the fit and adequate manifestation of His divine nature, He for our sakes descended, in respect of His human life, to the infinitely lower and poorer mode of existence which He assumed together with the nature of man"—Gifford.

"But made himself of no reputation." The literal translation of this is: "But emptied Himself." The question immediately arises, "Of what did the Lord Jesus empty Himself?"

In answering this question, one must use the greatest care. Human

2:7

19

attempts to define this emptying have often ended by stripping Christ of His attributes of deity. Some say, for instance, that when the Lord Jesus was on earth, He no longer had all-knowledge or all-power. He was no longer in all places at one and the same time. They say He voluntarily laid aside these attributes of deity when He came into the world as a Man. They say He was subject to the limitations of all men, that He became liable to error, and accepted the common opinions and myths of His day.

This we utterly deny. The Lord Jesus did not lay aside any of the attributes of God when He came into the world. He was still omniscient (all-knowing). He was still omnipresent (present in all places at one and the same time). He was still omnipotent (all-powerful). *What He did was to veil the glory of deity in a body of human flesh.* The glory was all there, though hidden, and it did shine forth on occasions, such as on the Mount of Transfiguration. There was no moment in His life on earth when He did not possess all the attributes of God.

> "Aside He threw His most divine array,
> And hid His Godhead in a veil of clay,
> And in that garb didst wondrous love display,
> Restoring what He never took away."

As mentioned before, one must use great care in explaining the words "He emptied Himself." The safest method is to let the succeeding expressions provide the explanation. He emptied Himself by taking the form of a servant and being made in the likeness of men. In other words, He emptied Himself by taking upon Himself something He never had before—HUMANITY. If He had been a mere man, this would not have been an act of emptying. We do not empty ourselves by being born into the world. But for God to become Man—that is the emptying of Himself. In fact, only God could do it.

"And took upon him the form of a servant." The incarnation and life of the Savior may be summarized by those lovely words of John 13:4: "He . . . laid aside his garments; and took a towel, and girded himself." The towel or apron is the badge of service. It was used by bond-servants. And it was used by the blessed Lord Jesus because He came "not to be ministered unto, but to minister, and to give his life a ransom for many" (Matthew 20:28).

But let us pause here to remind ourselves of the train of thought in this passage. There were contentions among the saints at Philippi. Paul exhorts them to have the mind of Christ. The argument, in brief, is that if Christians are willing to take the lowly place, to serve others, and to give their lives in sacrifice, there will be no quarrels. *People who are willing to die for others do not generally quarrel with them.*

Then we read that He "was made in the likeness of men," or better, "taking His place in the likeness of men"—Darby. The Lord was not *made;* He was not a created being. He always existed, but came into this world in the likeness of men. "The likeness of men" means "as a real Man." The humanity of the Lord is as real as His deity. He is true God and true Man. But what a mystery this is! No created mind will ever be able to understand it.

2:8

Each section of this passage describes the increasing depth of the humiliation of God's beloved Son. He was not only willing to leave the glory of heaven! He emptied Himself! He took the form of a Servant! He became Man! But now we read that He humbled Himself! There was no depth to which He would not stoop to save our guilty souls! Blessed be His glorious Name forever! He humbled Himself by becoming obedient unto death. This is marvelous in our eyes! He obeyed even though it cost Him His life. "Obedient unto death" means He obeyed to the end. Truly He was the merchant man who went and sold all that He had to buy the pearl of great price (Matthew 13:46). "Even the death of the cross." Death by crucifixion was the most shameful form of execution. It might be compared to the gallows, or the electric chair, or the gas chamber—reserved only for murderers. And that was the form of death reserved for heaven's Best when He came into this world. He was not allowed to die a natural death in bed. His was not to be an accidental death. He must die the shameful death of the cross.

2:9

Now there is an abrupt change. The previous verses describe what the Lord Jesus did. He took the path of self-renunciation. He did not seek a name for Himself. He humbled Himself. But now we turn to a consideration of what God has done. If the Savior humbled Himself, God has highly exalted Him. If He did not seek a name for Himself,

God has given Him a Name that is above every name. If He bent His knees in service to others, God has decreed that every knee shall bow to Him.

And what is the lesson in this for the Philippians—and for us? The lesson is that the way up is down. We should not exalt ourselves but be the servant of others, that God may exalt us in due time. God exalted Christ by raising Him from the dead and opening the heavens to receive Him back to His Own right hand. Not only that—God has given Him the Name that is above every name.

Scholars are divided as to what this Name is. Some say it is the name Jesus, which contains the Name of Jehovah. In Isaiah 45:22, 23, it is decreed that every knee will bow to the Name of Jehovah (God). Others feel that the Name which is above every name is simply a figurative way of saying the highest place in the universe, a position of supremacy and dominion. Both explanations are acceptable.

2:10   God was so completely satisfied with the redemptive work of Christ that He determined that every knee shall bow to Him—of beings in heaven, on the earth, and under the earth. This does not, of course, mean that all these beings will be saved. Those who do not willingly bow the knee to Him now will one day be compelled to do so. Those who will not be reconciled in the day of His grace will be subjugated in the day of His judgment.

2:11   In matchless grace, the Lord journeyed from glory to Bethlehem, to Gethsemane, and to Calvary. God, in return, will honor Him with universal homage and the universal acknowledgment of His Lordship. Those who have denied His claims will one day admit that they have played the fool, that they have greatly erred, and that Jesus of Nazareth was indeed the Lord of glory.

Before leaving this magnificent passage on the Person and work of the Lord Jesus, we should repeat that it was introduced in connection with a minor problem in the church at Philippi. The apostle Paul did not set out to write a treatise on the Lord. Rather, he was merely seeking to correct selfishness and party spirit in the saints. The cure of their condition is the mind of Christ. Paul brings the Lord into every situation. "Even in dealing with matters most delicate, distressing and distasteful, he is able to state truth in such striking beauty as to

make it appear like a precious jewel embedded in a clod of earth"—
Erdman.

PRACTICAL EXHORTATIONS (2:12-16)

Having set forth the example of Christ in such brilliant luster, the **2:12**
apostle is now ready to press home the exhortation based on it. The
Philippians had always obeyed Paul when he was present with them.
Much more now that he is absent, they should work out their own
salvation with fear and trembling.

Again we come to a passage of Scripture concerning which there
has been much confusion. At the outset, we should be very clear that
Paul is not teaching that salvation can be earned by works. Throughout
his writings, he repeatedly emphasizes that salvation is not by works
but by faith in the Lord Jesus Christ. What then does the verse mean?
(1) It may mean that we are to work out the salvation which God has
placed within us. God has given us eternal life as a free gift. We are to
live it out by lives of practical holiness. (2) Salvation here may mean
the solution of their problem at Philippi. They had been plagued with
squabbles and strife. The apostle has given them the remedy. Now they
are to apply the remedy by having the mind of Christ. Thus they would
work out their own salvation, or the solution of their difficulty. Dr.
C. I. Scofield agrees that the salvation spoken of here is not that of the
soul, but deliverance from the snares which would hinder the Christian
from doing the will of God. In a similar vein, Vine describes it as the
present entire experience of deliverance from evil. Salvation has many
different meanings in the New Testament. We have already noticed that
in chapter 1, verse 19, it means deliverance from prison. In chapter 1,
verse 28, it refers to the eventual salvation of our bodies from the very
presence of sin. The meaning in any particular case must be determined
in part, at least, by the context. We believe that in this passage salvation
means the solution of the problem that was vexing the Philippians, that
is, their contentions.

Now Paul reminds them that it is possible for them to work out **2:13**
their salvation because it is God Who works in them "both to will and

to do of his good pleasure." This means that it is God Who puts within us the wish or desire to do His will, in the first place. Then He also works in us the power to carry out the desire. Here again we have the wonderful merging of the divine and the human. In one sense, we are called upon to work out our salvation. In another sense, it is only God Who can enable us to do it. We must do our part, and God will do His. (However, this does not apply to the forgiveness of sins, or to the new birth. Redemption is wholly the work of God. We simply believe and enter in.)

2:14 As we do His good pleasure, we should do it without murmurings or questionings. "Not somehow but triumphantly." Murmurings and **2:15** disputings usually lead to graver offenses. By refraining from complaints and strifes, we may "be blameless and harmless" (sincere or guileless). To be blameless means that no charge can be sustained against a person. (See Daniel 6:4.) A blameless person may sin, but he apologizes, confesses, and makes it right whenever possible. To be harmless here means to be sincere or without guile.

"Children of God without blemish in the midst of a crooked and perverse generation" (A.S.V.). By lives without blemish, God's children will stand out all the more clearly against the dark background of this world. This leads Paul to think of them as lights in a dark night. The darker the night, the brighter the light appears. Christians are lights or light-bearers. They cannot create any light, but they can reflect the glory of the Lord so that others may see Jesus in them.

2:16 "Holding forth the word of life." As F. B. Meyer has said, "We are not only stars to shine but voices to speak." There should be the two-fold testimony of life and lips. If the Philippians fulfill these functions, the apostle knows he will have some ground for glorying in the day of Christ. He feels a responsibility not only to see souls saved but also to see them progressing in the Christian life. His ambition is to present every man perfect in Christ (Colossians 1:28). "The day of Christ" in this verse refers to the time of His return for His own and of the judgment of the believer's service (1:6, 10). If the Philippians are faithful in their labor for the Lord, it will be evident in that day that Paul's service had not been in vain.

24

THE EXAMPLE OF PAUL HIMSELF (2:17-18)

In this verse, the apostle uses a very beautiful illustration to describe **2:17** the service of the Philippians and of himself. He borrows the picture from the common practice among both Jews and heathen of pouring out a drink offering or libation over a sacrifice as it was being offered. He speaks of the Philippians as the offerers. Their faith is the sacrifice. Paul himself is the drink offering. He would be happy to be poured out in martyrdom on the sacrifice and service of their faith. "The apostle compares the self-sacrifice and energy of the Philippians with his own, magnifying theirs and minimizing his. They were both laying down their lives for the sake of the gospel, but their action he regards as the great sacrifice, and his as only the drink offering poured out upon it. Under this beauteous figure of speech, he speaks of his possible approaching death as a martyr"—Williams. If this should be his lot, he would rejoice and be glad that it should be so. In the same manner, the **2:18** Philippians should joy and rejoice with him. They should not look upon his possible martyrdom as a tragedy but congratulate him on such a glorious homegoing.

THE EXAMPLE OF TIMOTHY (2:19-24)

Up to this point, Paul has cited two examples of self-sacrificing love— **2:19** the Lord Jesus and himself. Both were willing to pour out their lives unto death. Two more examples of selflessness remain—Timothy and Epaphroditus. The apostle hopes to send Timothy to Philippi in the near future so that he may be comforted by news concerning them. Among Paul's companions, Timothy was unique in his unselfish care **2:20** for the spiritual condition of the Philippians. There was no one else whom Paul could send to them with the same confidence. This is a high commendation indeed for young Timothy! The others had become **2:21** engulfed in the ocean of their own private interests. They had become so engrossed with the cares of this life that they had no time for the things of Jesus Christ. Does this have a message for us today in our little world of homes, refrigerators, television sets, and other "things"?

(See Luke 8:14.)

2:22   Timothy was the apostle's child in the faith, and he played the part with true faithfulness. They knew "the proof of him," that is, his real worth, how that as a child serves his father, so Timothy served with

2:23   Paul in the work of preaching the gospel. Because Timothy had thus proved himself, Paul hoped to send him to the Philippians as soon as he learned the outcome of his appeal to Caesar. This is doubtless the apostle's meaning in the expression "so soon as I shall see how it will

2:24   go with me." He hopes that his appeal will be successful, and that he will be set free so that he might visit the Philippians once more.

THE EXAMPLE OF EPAPHRODITUS (2:25-30)

2:25   In the closing verses of the chapter, we see the mind of Christ in Epaphroditus. Whether this is the same man as the Epaphras of Colossians 4:12, we cannot be sure. At any rate, he lived in Philippi and was a messenger for the assembly there. Paul speaks of him as: (1) my brother; (2) my fellow-worker (A.S.V.); (3) my fellow-soldier. The first title speaks of affection, the second of hard work, and the third of conflict. We learn from this that he was a man who could work with others, and this is certainly a great essential in Christian life and service. It is one thing for a believer to work independently, having everything his own way. It is far more difficult to work with others, to play "second fiddle," to allow for individual differences, to submerge one's own desires and opinions for the good of the group. Let us be *fellow*-workers and *fellow*-soldiers!

   In addition, Paul speaks of him as "your messenger, and he that ministered to my wants." This gives us another valuable clue into his personality. He was willing to do common or menial work. So many today are only interested in work that is public and pleasant. How thankful we should be for those who carry on the routine work quietly and inconspicuously! By doing the hard work, Epaphroditus humbled himself. But God exalted him by recording his faithful service in Philippians 2 for all future generations to read.

2:26   The saints had sent Epaphroditus to help Paul—a journey of at least 700 miles. The faithful messenger took sick as a result; indeed, he came very close to death. This caused him grave concern—not the fact that he was so sick, but the fear that the saints might hear about it. If they did, they would reproach themselves for sending him on this journey and for thus endangering his life. Surely in Epaphroditus we see "a heart at leisure from itself." With many Christians it is an unfortunate habit to dwell at great length on their illnesses or operations. Too often this is but a manifestation of the hyphenated sins of the self-life: self-pity, self-occupation, self-display.

2:27 Epaphroditus had been sick near to death, but God had mercy on him. This section is valuable to us for the light it throws on the subject of divine healing. First of all, we learn that sickness is not always the result of sin. Here is a man who was sick because of the faithful discharge of his duties (see verse 30), ". . . for the work of Christ he was nigh unto death." Secondly, we learn that it is not always God's will to heal instantly and miraculously. It appears that Epaphroditus' illness was prolonged and his recovery gradual. (See also 2 Timothy 4:20; 3 John 2.) Thirdly, we learn that healing is a mercy from God and not something we can demand from Him as being our right.

Paul adds that God had mercy not only on Epaphroditus but also on himself, lest he "should have sorrow upon sorrow." The apostle already had considerable sorrow in connection with his imprisonment. If Epaphroditus had died, he would have had additional sorrow.

2:28 Now that Epaphroditus had recovered so well, Paul has sent him back home with great diligence (the more carefully). The Philippians would rejoice to have their beloved brother back again, and this would lessen Paul's sorrow also. **2:29** Not only should they receive Epaphroditus joyfully, but they should also respect this dear man of God. It is a great dignity and privilege to be engaged in the service of the Lord. The saints should recognize this, even when it concerns one with whom they are very familiar.

2:30 As mentioned previously, Epaphroditus' illness was directly connected with his tireless service for Christ. This is of great value in the eyes of the Lord. "It is better to burn out for Christ than to rust out." It is better to die in the service of Jesus than to be counted a mere statistic among those who die from illness or accident.

It is difficult to know exactly what Paul meant when he said, "To supply your lack of service toward me." Does this suggest that the Philippians had neglected Paul and that Epaphroditus had done what they should have done? This seems very unlikely, since it was the saints at Philippi who had sent Epaphroditus to Paul in the first place. Rather, we would suggest that their lack of service refers to their inability to visit Paul in person and to help him directly because of their distance from Rome. Instead of rebuking them, the apostle is merely stating that Epaphroditus did, as their representative, what they were unable to do in person.

When you are ready, complete Exam 1 by answering questions 11-20 on pages 31-33. (You should have already answered questions 1-10 as part of your study of lesson 1.)

PHILIPPIANS, COLOSSIANS and PHILEMON

Exam 1
Lessons 1, 2

Name_____

(print plainly)

Exam
Grade_____

Address _____

City_____ State _____ Zip Code _____ Class Number _____

Instructor _____

LESSON 1

In the blank space in the right-hand margin write the letter of the correct answer. (50 points)

1. Paul's first European convert on his second missionary journey was
   a. a man from Macedonia
   b. a woman from Asia Minor
   c. a slave girl from Philippi
   d. a retired soldier from Rome   _____

2. Paul's epistle to the Philippians is one of the
   a. sternest he ever wrote
   b. most personal of all his writings
   c. most complex and difficult of all his letters
   d. most theological and controversial he ever penned   _____

3. In the New Testament church, as reflected at Philippi,
   a. a bishop presided over several churches
   b. a local church had one pastor and numerous deacons
   c. a local church had more than one bishop
   d. the bishop was always regarded as the ranking official in the local church   _____

4. Paul's love for the Philippians is very remarkable in view of
   a. their neglect of him once he became a prisoner
   b. the welcome they had given to the enemies of the gospel
   c. the natural coldness and formality of his disposition
   d. his Jewish birth and background   _____

5. Paul prayed for three things on behalf of the Philippians. Of those mentioned below, the item *NOT* specifically prayed for by him was that they might
   a. be delivered from harm and danger
   b. have abounding and enlightened love
   c. be able to discriminate between right and wrong
   d. be fruitful in all Christian virtue _____

6. As a result of Paul's imprisonment
   a. Caesar had become a Christian
   b. many Christians had been emboldened to witness for Christ
   c. a fresh persecution had broken out against the Church
   d. the work of evangelism in Europe had come almost to a standstill _____

7. Paul was expecting
   a. to be set at liberty soon
   b. to be executed shortly
   c. to be detained in prison for many years to come
   d. to be placed under house arrest soon instead of being kept in the main Roman prison _____

8. Paul's attitude towards death was one of
   a. natural shrinking and fear
   b. stoical resolution and indifference
   c. eager anticipation
   d. wavering between hope and despair _____

9. The doctrine of soul sleep
   a. can be supported from Paul's letter to the Philippians
   b. is unscriptural because the Bible teaches that, at death, a person's soul is completely extinguished
   c. is unscriptural because it is the spirit that sleeps at death, not the soul
   d. is unscriptural because in Scripture "sleep" at the time of death is related to the body, not the soul _____

10. In the face of opposition to the gospel, Paul pleads for
    a. compromise
    b. fearlessness
    c. surrender
    d. caution _____

WHAT DO YOU SAY?

Fill in the blank in the following statement after weighing your life and your goals in the presence of God.

For to me to live is _____ and to die is _____.

LESSON 2

11. Paul lists four reasons why Christians ought to be able to get along one with another in happy harmony. These are: *(5 points)*

a. _____

b. _____

c. _____

d. _____

In the blank space in the right-hand margin write the letter of the correct answer. (45 points)

12. The antidote to "strife" and "vain glory" is to
   a. retire from the world into some kind of monastic or hermit life
   b. always give in when challenged or opposed
   c. put others and their interests before ourselves and our interests
   d. accept some form of authoritarian government in the local church

   _____

13. As rendered in the American Standard Version, the statement concerning the Lord Jesus that He "thought it not robbery to be equal with God" means that He
   a. resembled God
   b. was equal to God before His incarnation but not afterwards
   c. had to fight for the full recognition of His Deity but, since He was God, He was within His rights in so doing
   d. was equal with God but did not consider it a thing to be grasped after at all costs

   _____

14. When the Lord Jesus "emptied Himself" He
    a. laid aside His glory
    b. veiled His glory in a human body
    c. put off His divine attributes
    d. became subject to all the limitations of humanity   _____

15. In discussing the Lord's great stoop from heaven to earth, Paul
    had a practical aim in mind. This aim was to
    a. silence certain false teachers at Philippi who were teaching
       that Jesus was not really God at all
    b. lay the foundation for the Christology of the New Testa-
       ment
    c. wean the Christians at Philippi away from Emperor worship
    d. urge humility and self sacrifice upon the believers so that
       quarreling would become impossible   _____

16. The "name which is above every name" is
    a. the name Jesus assumed Himself upon His ascension to
       Glory
    b. the name God has bestowed upon His Son
    c. the name that no man knows or can know, the name of
       mystery, the name He will bear forever in private intimacy
       with His Father
    d. the name He claimed for Himself over and over again when
       contending with His critics who challenged His claim to
       Deity   _____

17. Paul told the Philippians they were to "work out their own
    salvation." This
    a. is characteristic of Paul who consistently taught that salva-
       tion is by our own good works
    b. contradicts much of Paul's teaching elsewhere in the New
       Testament where he emphasizes that salvation is by faith,
       not by works
    c. implies that although we are saved by faith we are kept
       thereafter by our own good works
    d. may have nothing to do with the soul at all since the word
       "salvation" has different meanings in various places in the
       New Testament   _____

18. Paul makes mention of "the day of Christ," an expression which refers to the day when
   a. Christ will judge the world
   b. Christ will return for His own and will judge their service
   c. Christ was born in Bethlehem
   d. the present age of grace began   _____

19. Timothy is used by Paul as an example of
   a. selfless service
   b. patience in sickness
   c. boldness in witness
   d. victory over a contentious spirit   _____

20. Epaphroditus teaches us that
   a. the only work God prizes is that which is of a public nature
   b. affection, hard work and conflict ought to mark out the Christian
   c. God always heals the sick when we have boldness to demand it of Him and believe that He will
   d. the Christian life is one free from hardship and suffering   _____

WHAT DO YOU SAY?

How has this lesson helped you put right any difference you might have had with a fellow Christian?

_____

_____

_____

_____

_____

Pitfalls Along the Way

Philippians 3:1-21

I. Exhortation to rejoice (v. 1a).

II. Warning against false teachers (vv. 1b-2).

III. Legal righteousness and divine righteousness contrasted (vv. 3-9).

IV. The aim of the Christian (vv. 10, 11).

V. The process of achieving it (vv. 12-16).

VI. The example to follow (v. 17).

VII. The example to avoid (vv. 18, 19).

VIII. The heavenly citizenship and hope of the believer (vv. 20, 21).

REJOICE! BEWARE! (3:1-2)

When Paul says, "Finally, my brethren," he does not mean that he is about to close his epistle. The literal meaning is, "As for the rest. . . ." The same word is used again in chapter 4, verse 8.   **3:1**

He exhorts them to "rejoice in the Lord." The Christian can always find real joy in the Lord, no matter what his circumstances may be. "The source of all his singing is high in heaven above." Nothing can really affect his joy unless it first robs him of his Savior, and this clearly is impossible. Natural happiness is affected by pain, sorrow, sickness, poverty, and tragedy. But Christian joy rides high over all the billows of his life. Proof of this is found in the fact that Paul gives this exhortation from prison. Surely we can take the advice from such a man as he!

He does not find it irksome to repeat himself to the Philippians because he knows it is for their safety. But how does he repeat himself? Does this refer to the preceding expression where he urges them to rejoice in the Lord? Or does it mean the verses to follow where he warns them against the Judaizers? We believe that the latter is in view. Three times in verse 2 he uses the word "beware." To use the repetition is not tiresome for him, but for them it is a true safeguard.

3:2   They are to beware of dogs, of evil workers, and of the concision. We believe that all three expressions refer to the same group of men— false teachers who sought to put Christians under the laws of Judaism and who taught that righteousness could be obtained by law-keeping and ritualism. First of all, they were dogs. In the Bible, dogs are unclean animals. The term was used by Jews to describe Gentiles. In eastern countries, dogs were homeless creatures, living in the streets and scrounging food as best they could. Here Paul turns the tables and applies the term to those Jewish false teachers who were seeking to corrupt the church. They were really the ones who were living on the outside, trying to exist on rituals and ceremonies. They were "picking up the crumbs when they might sit down to a feast."

Secondly, they were evil workers. Professing to be true believers, they gained admission into Christian fellowships in order to spread their false teachings. The results of their work could only be evil.

Then Paul also calls them the concision. This is an ironical term to describe their attitude toward circumcision. Doubtless they insisted that a person must be circumcised in order to be saved. But all they meant by this was the physical, literal act of circumcision. They were not at all concerned with its spiritual meaning. Circumcision speaks of death to the flesh. It means that the claims of the fleshly nature should not be allowed. While they insisted on the literal act of circumcision, they gave full rein to the flesh. There was no heart acknowledgment that the flesh had been put to death at the cross. In calling them "the concision" Paul was saying that they were mere mutilators of the flesh, who did not distinguish between the ceremony and its underlying meaning.

36

LEGAL RIGHTEOUSNESS OR TRUE RIGHTEOUSNESS? (3:3-9)

In contrast with these, Paul states that we (true believers) are the cir- **3:3**
cumcision—not those who are born of Jewish parents or who have been
literally circumcised, but those who realize that the flesh profits
nothing, that man cannot do anything in his own strength to win God's
smile of approval. Then Paul gives three characteristics of those who
are the true circumcision:

1. They worship God in (or by) the Spirit. That is, theirs is a true
   spiritual worship, and not one of mere ceremonies. In true worship, a person enters into the presence of God by faith and pours
   out his love, praise, adoration, and homage. Soulish worship, on
   the other hand, is occupied with beautiful buildings and ecclesiastical furniture, with elaborate ceremonies, with brocaded priestly
   garments, and with whatever appeals to the emotions.

2. Members of the true circumcision rejoice in Christ Jesus, or better,
   "they glory in Christ Jesus." He alone is the ground of their
   boasting. They do not pride themselves in their personal attainments, in their cultural background, or in their faithfulness to
   sacraments.

3. They have no confidence in the flesh. They do not think that they
   can be saved through fleshly efforts in the first place or be kept by
   their own strength thereafter. They do not expect any good from
   their Adam nature and are therefore not disappointed when they
   find none.

As Paul thought of how these men boasted in their fleshly advan- **3:4**
tages and attainments, a smile doubtless formed on his lips. If they
could boast, how much more could he! In the next two verses, he
shows how that to a pre-eminent degree he possessed those natural
assets in which man normally glories. "He seemed to have belonged to
almost every kind of aristocracy which excites the dreams and kindles
the aspirations of men." Concerning these two verses, Arnot has said:
"The whole stock-in-trade of the self-righteous Pharisee is inventoried
here. He delights to display the filthy rags and make a show of them
openly."

You will notice that Paul speaks of: Pride of ancestry (v. 5a);

pride of orthodoxy (v. 5b); pride of activity (v. 6a); and pride of morality (v. 6b).

3:5 Here, then, is the list of Paul's natural and fleshly advantages: *Circumcised the eighth day*—this means that he was a Jew by birth, and not a convert to Judaism. *Of the stock of Israel*—that is, a member of God's chosen earthly people. *Of the tribe of Benjamin*—a tribe that was considered a leader (Judges 5:14), and the one that gave Israel its first king. *A Hebrew of the Hebrews*—this may mean that both parents were Jewish, or that he belonged to that segment of the nation that had held onto its original language, customs, and usages. *As touching the law, a Pharisee*—the Pharisees had remained orthodox, whereas the Sadducees

3:6 had abandoned the doctrine of the resurrection. *Concerning zeal, persecuting the church*—Paul sincerely thought that he had been doing God's service when he had attempted to wipe out the "sect" of Christians. He saw in it a threat to his own religion and therefore felt he must exterminate it. *Touching the righteousness which is in the law, blameless*—this cannot mean that Paul had perfectly kept the law. He confesses in Romans 7:9, 10 that such was not the case. He speaks of himself as being blameless, not sinless. We can only conclude that when Paul had violated any part of the law, he was careful to bring the sacrifice required. In other words, he had been a stickler in seeking to observe the rules of Judaism to the letter. Thus, as to birth, pedigree, orthodoxy, zeal, and personal righteousness, Saul of Tarsus was an outstanding man.

3:7 But now the apostle makes the great renunciation. He here gives us his own "Profit and Loss Statement." On one side he lists the abovementioned items, the things that had been gain to him. On the other side he writes the single word "Christ." They all amount to nothing when compared with the treasure which he had found in Christ. He counted them loss for Christ. "All financial gain, all material gain, all physical gain, all intellectual gain, all moral gain, all religious gain—all these are no gains at all compared with the Great Gain"—King. As long as he trusted in these things, he could never have been saved. And once he was saved, they no longer meant anything to him because he had seen the glory of the Lord, and all other glories seemed like nothing in comparison.

In coming to Christ for salvation, the apostle had renounced all 3:8
things and counted them to be worthless when compared to the excellency of the knowledge of Christ Jesus, his Lord. "The excellency of
the knowledge" is a Hebrew expression for "the excellent knowledge"
or "the surpassing worth of knowing." Ancestry, nationality, culture,
prestige, education, religion, personal attainments—all these the apostle
abandoned as grounds for boasting. Indeed, he counted them as dung
or refuse in order that he might win (or gain) Christ.

Although the present tense is used in this verse and in the one
following, Paul is looking back primarily to the time of his conversion.
In order to gain Christ, he had had to turn his back on the things which
he had always been taught to prize most highly. If he were to have
Christ as his gain, he had to say good-by to his mother's religion, his
father's heritage, and his own personal attainments. And so he did! He
completely severed his ties with Judaism as a hope of salvation. In
doing so, he was disinherited by his relatives, disowned by his former
friends, and persecuted by his fellow countrymen. He literally suffered
the loss of all things when he became a Christian. Because the present
tense is used in verse 8, it sounds as if Paul were still seeking to gain
Christ. Actually, of course, he had won Christ when he first acknowledged Him as Lord and Savior. But the present tense indicates that this
is still his attitude; he still counts all else as rubbish when compared to
the value of knowing the Lord Jesus. The great desire of his heart is,
"That Christ may be my gain." Not gold, or silver, or religious reputation, but Christ.

"And be found in him." Here again it sounds as if Paul were still 3:9
trying to be found in Christ. The fact of the matter is that he is looking
back to the tremendous decision which faced him before he was saved.
Was he willing to abandon his own efforts to earn salvation, and simply
trust in Christ? He had made his choice. He had abandoned all else in
order to be found in Christ. The moment he believed on the Lord Jesus,
he stood in a new position before God. No longer was he seen as a child
of sinful Adam, but now he is seen IN CHRIST, enjoying all the favor
which the Lord Jesus enjoys before God the Father.

Likewise he had renounced the filthy rags of his own self-
righteousness, which he had sought to win by keeping the law, and had

chosen the righteousness of God which is bestowed on everyone who receives the Savior. Righteousness is here spoken of as a garment or covering. Man needs righteousness in order to stand before God in favor. But man cannot produce it. And so, in grace, God gives His own righteousness to those who receive His Son as Lord and Savior. "He (God) hath made him (Christ) to be sin for us, who knew no sin; that we might be made the righteousness of God in him" (2 Corinthians 5:21).

Again we would like to emphasize that verses 8 and 9 do not suggest that Paul had not yet received the righteousness of God. On the contrary, this became his possession when he was regenerated on the road to Damascus. But the present tense simply indicates that the results of that important event continued up to the present and that Paul still considered Christ to be worth far more than anything he had given up.

THE AIM OF THE CHRISTIAN LIFE (3:10-16)

3:10   As we read the words in this verse, we come to the supreme emotion of the apostle's life. F. B. Meyer calls it "The Soul's Quest for the Personal Christ."

The most frequent treatment of this passage is to spiritualize it. By this it is meant that suffering, death, and resurrection are not to be taken literally. Rather, they are used to describe certain spiritual experiences, such as mental suffering, dying to self, and living the resurrected life, etc. However, we would like to suggest that the passage should be taken literally. Paul is saying that he wants to live as Christ lived. Did the Lord Jesus suffer? Then Paul wants to suffer too. Did the Lord Jesus die? Then Paul wants to die by martyrdom in his service for Christ. Did the Lord Jesus rise from among the dead? Then Paul wishes to do the same. He realized that the servant is not above his Master. Thus, he desired to follow Christ in His suffering, death, and resurrection. He does not say that all must adopt this view, but for him there could be no other pathway.

"That I may know him." Here, to know Him means to gain

practical day-by-day acquaintance with Him in such an intimate way that the apostle himself would become more Christ-like. He wants the life of Christ to be reproduced in him. "And the power of his resurrection." The power that raised the Lord from the dead is set forth in Scripture as the greatest display of power that the universe has ever seen (Ephesians 1:19-20). It would seem as if all the hosts of evil were determined to keep His body in the tomb. God's mighty power defeated this infernal army by raising the Lord Jesus from the dead on the third day. This same power is placed at the disposal of all believers (Ephesians 1:19), to be appropriated by faith. Paul is here stating his ambition to experience this power in his life and testimony. "And the fellowship of his sufferings." One must have divine strength in order to suffer for Christ. That is why "the power of his resurrection" is placed before "the fellowship of his sufferings."

In the life of the Lord, suffering preceded glory. So then it must be in the life of Paul. He must share Christ's sufferings. He realized, of course, that there would be nothing of an atoning value in his sufferings, as there was in Christ's, but he knew, too, that it would be inconsistent for him to live in luxury and ease in a world where his Lord was rejected and scourged. "He was not contented to share the triumph of Olivet; he wanted to feel something of the pang and chill and loneliness of Gethsemane"—Jowett. "Being made comformable unto his death." As mentioned previously, this is usually explained as meaning that Paul wanted to live the crucified life, to die practically to sin, self, and the world. But we feel that such an interpretation robs the passage of its shocking force. It means that, but much more.

Paul was a passionately devoted follower of the One Who died on the cross of Calvary. Not only that, he was present when the first martyr of the Christian church died; indeed, he was an accomplice in murdering him. We believe that Paul was actually ánxious to pour out his life in the same way. Perhaps he would have felt embarrassed to meet Stephen in heaven if he had come by any more comfortable route than martyrdom.

"Many Christians are satisfied with expenditure in which there is no 'shedding of blood.' They give away what they can easily spare. Their gifts are detached things, and the surrender of them necessitates no bleeding. They engage in sacrifice as long as it does not involve life: when the really vital is demanded, they are not to be found. They are prominent at all triumphant entries, and they willingly spend a little money on gay decorations—on banners and palm branches; but when 'Hurrahs' and 'Hosannas' change into ominous murmurs and threats, and Calvary comes into sight, they steal away into safe seclusion.

"But here is an Apostle who joyfully anticipates this supreme and critical demand. He is almost impatient at his own dribblings of blood-energy in the service of the kingdom! He is eager if need be to pour it out"—Jowett.

It was in a similar vein that Hudson Taylor wrote: "There is a needs-be for us to give *ourselves* for the life of the world. . . . Fruit-bearing involves cross-bearing. 'Except a corn of wheat fall into the ground and die, it abideth alone.' We know how the Lord Jesus became fruitful—not by bearing His cross only, but by dying on it. Do we know much of fellowship with Him in this? There are not two Christs—an easy-going Christ for easy-going Christians, and a suffering, toiling Christ for exceptional believers. There is only one Christ. Are we willing to abide in Him and so to bear fruit?"

"The knowledge of Christ in glory was the supreme desire of Paul's heart, and this desire could never exist without producing an intense longing to reach Him in the place where He is. Hence the heart that longs after Him instinctively turns to the path by which He reached that place in glory, and earnestly desires to reach Him in that place by the very path which He trod. The heart asks, 'How did *He* reach that glory? Was it not through resurrection? And did not sufferings and death necessarily precede resurrection?' Then the heart says, 'Nothing would please me so well as to reach Him in resurrection glory by the very path which took *Him* there.' It is the martyr spirit. Paul wanted to tread as a martyr the pathway of suffering and death, that he might reach resurrection and glory by the same path as the blessed One who had won his heart"—C. A. Coates.

3:11   Here again we are faced with a problem of interpretation. Are we to take this verse literally, or are we to spiritualize it? Various explanations have been offered, the principal of which are as follows:

1. Paul was not sure that he would be raised from the dead, so he was straining every muscle to insure his participation in the resurrection. Such a view is impossible. Paul always taught that resurrection was by grace and not by human works. In addition, he expressed the definite confidence that he would participate in the resurrection (2 Corinthians 5:1-8).

2. Paul was not speaking of a physical, literal resurrection at all, but was referring to his desire to live the resurrection life while still here on earth. Perhaps the majority of the commentators hold this view.

3. Paul was here talking about literal, physical resurrection, but he was not expressing any doubt about his participation in it. Rather he was saying that he was not concerned about the sufferings that might lie before him en route to the resurrection. He was willing to undergo severe trials and persecutions, if that was what lay between the present time and the resurrection. The expression "if by any means" does not necessarily express doubt (see Acts 27:12; Romans 1:10; 11:14), but strong desire or expectation that does not count the cost.

We agree with the third interpretation. The apostle wanted to be conformed to Christ. Since Christ had suffered, had died, and had been raised from among the dead, Paul wanted nothing better than this for himself. We fear that our own desire for comfort, luxury, and ease often causes us to remove the sharp, cutting edges of some of these Bible verses. Would it not be safer to take them at their face value—literally—unless that sense is impossible in the light of the rest of the Bible?

Before leaving this verse, we should notice that Paul is not speaking of the resurrection *of* the dead, as given in the Authorized Version. It is more correctly translated "the resurrection *from among* the dead." This is not a resurrection of all the dead. Rather, it describes a resurrection in which some will be raised, but others will remain in the grave. We know from 1 Thessalonians 4:13-18 and 1 Corinthians 15:

51-57 that believers will be raised at the coming of Christ for His saints, but the rest of the dead will not be raised until after Christ's 1000-year reign on earth (Revelation 20:5).

3:12   Of course, the apostle did not consider that he was already made perfect. "Perfect" here refers not to the resurrection in the previous verse, but to the whole subject of conformity to Christ. He had no idea that it was possible to achieve a state of sinlessness or to arrive at a condition in life where no further progress could be achieved. He realized that "satisfaction is the grave of progress." Thus he pressed on in order that the purpose for which the Lord had saved him might be fulfilled in him. The apostle had been apprehended by Christ Jesus on the road to Damascus. What was the purpose of this momentous meeting? It was that Paul might thereafter be a pattern-saint, that God might show through him what Christ can do in a human life. Had this purpose been achieved in his life? No, he was not yet perfectly conformed to Christ. The process was still going on, and Paul was deeply exercised that this work of God's grace might continue and deepen.

3:13   This man who had learned to be content with whatever material things he had (4:11) never could be content with his spiritual attainments. He did not count himself to have "arrived," as we would say today. What then did he do? "This one thing I do," he said. He was a man of single purpose. He had one aim and ambition. In this he resembled David, who said, "One thing have I desired of the Lord." "Forgetting those things which are behind." This would mean not only his sins and failures but also his natural privileges, attainments, and successes which he had described earlier in this chapter, and even his spiritual triumphs. "And reaching forth unto those things which are before," namely, the privileges and responsibilities of the Christian life, whether worship, service, or the personal development of Christian character.

3:14   Looking upon himself as a runner in a race, Paul describes himself as exerting every effort toward "the mark for the prize of the high calling of God in Christ Jesus." The mark is the finish line at the end of a race track. The prize is the award which is presented to the winner. Here the mark would be the finish of life's race, and perhaps more particularly the judgment seat of Christ. The prize would be the crown

44

of righteousness which Paul elsewhere describes as the prize for those who have run well (2 Timothy 4:7). "The high calling of God in Christ Jesus" includes all the purposes that God had in mind in saving us. It includes salvation, conformity to Christ, joint-heirship with Him, a home in heaven, and numberless other spiritual blessings.

As many as are perfect, that is, full-grown or mature, should share **3:15** Paul's willingness to suffer and die for Christ and to bend every effort in the quest for likeness to the Lord Jesus. This is the mature view of the Christian faith. Some would call it extreme or radical or fanatical. But the apostle states that those who are full-grown will see that this is the only sane, logical, reasonable response to the One Who shed His life-blood for them on Calvary.

"If in any thing ye be otherwise minded, God shall reveal even this unto you." Here Paul realizes that not all will agree with him in adopting such a dangerous philosophy. But he expresses the confidence that if a person is really willing to know the truth of the matter, God will show it to him. The reason we have such an easy-going, complacent Christianity today is because we do not want to know the truth; we are not willing to obey the demands of ideal Christianity. God is willing to show the truth to those who are willing to follow it.

Then the apostle adds that, in the meantime, we should live up to **3:16** whatever light the Lord has given us. It would not do to mark time until we came to a fuller knowledge of what is required of us as Christians. While we wait for the Lord to reveal the full implications of the cross to us, we should obey whatever measure of light we have received.

TWO OPPOSITE EXAMPLES (3:17-19)

Now the apostle turns to exhortation, first by encouraging the Philip- **3:17** pians to be followers, or imitators together of himself. It is a tribute to his exemplary life that he could ever write such words. We often hear the expression in jest, "Do as I say, but not as I do." Not so the apostle! He could hold up his own life as a model of wholehearted devotion to Christ and to His cause.

"Paul considered himself the recipient of God's mercy that he might be a 'pattern'; thus his whole life, subsequent to his conversion, was dedicated to presenting to others an outline sketch of what a Christian should be. God saved Paul in order that he might show by the example of his conversion that what Jesus Christ did for him He can and will do for others. Was not this the special object our Lord had in view in extending His mercy to you and me? I believe He has saved us to be a pattern to all future believers. Are we serving as examples of those who have been saved by His grace? May it be so!"—Lehman Strauss.

"And mark them that so walk even as ye have us for an example." This refers to any others who were living the same kind of life as Paul. It does not mean to mark them out disapprovingly, as would be the case in the next verse, but to observe them with a view to following in their steps.

3:18   Just as the preceding verse describes those whom believers should follow, the next two tells of those whom we should not follow. The apostle does not identify these men specifically—whether they were the Judaizing false teachers mentioned in verse 2, or whether they were professed Christian teachers who turned liberty into license, and used grace as a pretext for sin, he does not say. Paul had warned the saints about these men previously, and he does so again with tears. But why the tears in the midst of such a stern denunciation? Because of the harm these men did among the churches of God. Because of the lives they ruined. Because of the reproach they brought on the Name of Christ. Because they were obscuring the true meaning of the cross. Yes, but also because true love weeps even when denouncing the enemies of the cross of Christ, just as the Lord Jesus wept over the murderous city of Jerusalem.

3:19   These men were destined to eternal perdition. This does not mean annihilation, but the judgment of God in the lake of fire forever and ever. Their god was their belly. All their activities, even their professed religious service, were directed toward the purchase of food (and perhaps drink) for the gratification of their bodily appetite. Concerning these men, F. B. Meyer finely wrote, "There is no chapel in their life. It is all kitchen." Their glory was their shame. They boasted in the very things they should have been ashamed of—their nakedness and their immoral behavior. They were occupied with earthly things. For them, the important things in life were food, clothing, honor, comfort, and pleasure. Eternal issues and heavenly things did not disturb their grovelling in the muck of this world. They carried on as if they were going to live on the earth forever.

THE BELIEVER'S CITIZENSHIP AND HOPE (3:20-21)

The apostle now contrasts the heavenly-minded attitude of the true **3:20** believer.

At the time the epistle was written, Philippi was a colony of Rome (Acts 16:12). The people there were citizens of Rome, enjoying its protection and privileges. But they were also citizens of their local government. Against this backdrop, the apostle reminds the believers that their citizenship (conversation) is in heaven. Moffatt translates it, "But we are a colony of heaven." This does not, of course, mean that Christians are not also citizens of earthly countries. Other Scriptures clearly teach that we are to be subject to governments because they are ordained by God (Romans 13:1-7). Indeed, believers should be obedient to the government in all matters that are not expressly forbidden by the Lord. The Philippians owed allegiance to the local magistrates, and also to the Emperor in Rome. So believers have responsibilities to earthly governments, but their first loyalty is to the Lord in heaven. Not only are we citizens of heaven, but we look (wait) for a Savior from heaven! "The word translated 'wait' is the strongest that any language could supply to express the earnest expectation of something believed to be imminent. According to Bloomfield, 'it signifies properly to thrust forward the head and neck as in anxious expectation of hearing or seeing something' "—Sir Robert Anderson.

When the Lord Jesus comes from heaven, He will change these **3:21** bodies of ours. The translation "our vile body" is better rendered "the body of our humiliation." There is nothing vile or evil about the human body in itself. The evil lies in the wrong uses to which it is put. But it is a body of humiliation. It is subject to wrinkles, scars, age, suffering, sickness, and death. "It limits us and cramps us!" The Lord will change

47

it into a body of glory. The full extent of the meaning of this we do not know. It will no longer be subject to decay or death. It will no longer be subject to the limitations of time or of natural barriers. It will be a real body, yet perfectly suited to conditions in heaven. It will be like the resurrection body of the Lord Jesus.

This does not mean that we will all have the same physical appearance. The Lord Jesus was distinctly recognizable after His resurrection, and doubtless each individual will have his own individual physical identity in eternity. Also, this passage does not teach that we shall be like the Lord Jesus as far as the attributes of God are concerned. We shall never have all knowledge or all power; neither shall we be in all places at one and the same time. But we shall be morally like the Lord Jesus. We shall be forever free from sin.

As Erdman has pointed out, this passage does not give us enough to satisfy our curiosity, but it is enough to inspire comfort and to stimulate hope.

"According to the working whereby he is able even to subdue all things unto himself." The transformation of our bodies will be accomplished by the same divine power which the Lord will later use to subdue all things unto Himself. In Hebrews 7:25 we learn that He is "able to save." Hebrews 2:18 states that He is "able to succour." Jude 24 reminds us that He is "able to keep." Now in this verse we learn that He is "able to subdue." "This God is our God for ever and ever: he will be our guide even unto death" (Psalm 48:14).

When you have mastered this lesson, take the first part of Exam 2 (covering lesson 3), questions 1-10 on pages 61-63 (right after lesson 4).

Lesson Four

Victorious Living

Philippians 4:1-23

I. Exhortation to steadfastness (v. 1).
II. Appeal for reconciliation of two sisters (vv. 2, 3).
III. Various exhortations to:
   a. rejoice (v. 4).
   b. forbear (v. 5).
   c. pray and give thanks (vv. 6, 7).
   d. think positively and purely (vv. 8, 9).
IV. The apostle acknowledges a gift from Philippi (vv. 10-20).
V. Closing greetings (vv. 21-23).

STAND FAST! (4:1)

On the basis of the wonderful hope which the apostle had set before **4:1** the minds of the believers in the previous verse, he now exhorts them to stand fast in the Lord. The student will notice that this verse is filled with endearing names for the believers. First of all, Paul calls them his brethren. But not only his brethren, but his brethren beloved. Then he adds the thought that he longs for them, that is, he longs to be with them again. Further, he speaks of them as his joy and crown. Doubtless he means that they are his joy at the present time and will be his crown at the judgment seat of Christ. Finally, he closes the verse with the expression "my dearly beloved." The apostle really loved people, and doubtless this is one of the secrets of his effectiveness in the work of the Lord.

QUIT SQUABBLING (4:2-3)

4:2 It is clear that Euodias and Syntyche were sisters in the assembly at Philippi who were having difficulty getting along together. We are not given details as to the cause of their disagreement, and perhaps it is just as well.

The apostle uses the word "beseech" twice to show that the exhortation is addressed just as much to the one as to the other. Paul urges them to be of the same mind in the Lord. It is impossible for us to be united in all things in daily life, but, as far as the things of the Lord are concerned, it is possible for us to submerge our petty, personal differences in order that the Lord might be magnified and His work might be advanced.

4:3 There is considerable speculation as to the identity of the true yoke-fellow whom Paul addresses in this verse. Timothy and Luke have both been suggested, but we feel that Epaphroditus is probably the person spoken of. At any rate, he is exhorted to help these women who had labored with Paul in the gospel. We take it that these women were Euodias and Syntyche, and that the apostle Paul is giving what experience has proved to be sound advice. Oftentimes when two people have been quarreling, the quarrel can best be settled by taking it to an independent third party—someone with mature, spiritual judgment. It is not that he acts arbitrarily in the case and hands down a decision, but rather that by appealing to the Word of God, he is able to show the contending persons the Scriptural solution to their problem.

Care should be taken in interpreting the expression "they labored with me in the gospel." By no stretch of the imagination can this be taken to mean that they preached the gospel with the apostle Paul. There are many ways in which women can labor in the gospel—by hospitality to the servants of Christ, by home visitation, by teaching younger women and children—without assuming a ministry of public teaching or preaching. (1 Cor. 14:34, 35; 1 Tim. 2:9-15)

Another co-laborer named Clement is mentioned in this verse. Nothing further is known of him with certainty. Then Paul mentions the rest of his fellow workers whose names are in the book of life. This is a lovely way of expressing the eternal and unspeakable blessedness that attaches to faith in Christ and service for Him.

WATCH YOUR ATTITUDES (4:4-9)

Turning now to the entire church, Paul repeats the favorite exhortation. **4:4** The secret of his exhortation is found in the words "in the Lord." No matter how dark the circumstances of life may be, it is always possible for the Christian to rejoice in the Lord.

"Christian joy is a mood independent of our immediate circumstances. If it were dependent on our surroundings, then, indeed, it would be as uncertain as an unprotected candle burning in a gusty night. One moment the candle burns clear and steady, the next moment the blaze leaps to the very edge of the wick, and affords little or no light. But Christian joy has no relationship to the transient settling of the life, and therefore it is not the victim of the passing day. At one time my conditions arrange themselves like a sunny day in June; a little later they rearrange themselves like a gloomy day in November. One day I am at the wedding; the next day I stand by an open grave. One day, in my ministry, I win ten converts for the Lord; and then, for a long stretch of days, I never win one. Yes, the days are as changeable as the weather, and yet the Christian joy can be persistent. Where lies the secret of its gracious persistency?

"Here is the secret. 'Lo! I am with you *all the days.*' In all the changing days, 'He changeth not, neither is weary.' He is no fair-weather Companion, leaving me when the year grows dark and cold. He does not choose my days of prosperous festival, though not to be found in my days of impoverishment and defeat. He does not show Himself only when I wear a garland, and hide Himself when I wear a crown of thorns. He is with me 'all the days'—the prosperous days and the days of adversity; days when the funeral bell is tolling, and days when the wedding bell is ringing. 'All the days.' The day of life—the day of death —the day of judgment"—Jowett.

4:5 Now Paul urges them to let their moderation be known to all men. Moderation has also been translated yieldedness, gentleness, sweet reasonableness, and willingness to give up one's own way. As Erdman has said, however, the difficult part of the verse is found in the expression "unto all men." The difficulty does not lie in understanding what is meant, but in obeying the precept "unto all men." "The Lord is at hand" may mean that the Lord is now present, or that the Lord's coming is near. Both are true, though we favor the latter view.

4:6 It is now well-known that the word "careful" in this verse should be translated "anxious." Is it really possible for a Christian to be anxious for nothing? It is possible as long as we have the resource of believing prayer. The rest of the verse goes on to explain how our lives can be free from sinful fretting. Everything should be taken to the Lord in prayer. "Everything" means *everything*. There is nothing too great or too small for His loving care.

Prayer is both an act and an atmosphere. We come to the Lord at specific times and bring specific requests before Him. But it is also possible to live in an atmosphere of prayer. It is possible that the mood of our life should be a prayerful mood. Perhaps the word "prayer" in this verse signifies the over-all attitude of our life, whereas supplication specifies the specific requests which we bring to the Lord. But then we should notice that our requests should be made known to God with thanksgiving. Someone has summarized the verse as saying that we should be "anxious in nothing, prayerful in everything, thankful for anything."

4:7 If these attitudes characterize our lives, the peace of God which passes all understanding shall keep our hearts and minds through Christ Jesus. The peace of God is a sense of holy repose and complacency which floods the soul of the believer when he is leaning hard upon God.

> "Stayed upon Jehovah
> Hearts are fully blessed;
> Finding, as He promised,
> Perfect peace and rest."

This peace passes all understanding. People of the world cannot understand it at all, and even Christians possessing it find a wonderful element of mystery about it. They are surprised at their own lack of anxiety in the face of tragedy or adverse circumstances. This peace garrisons the heart and the thought life. What a needed tonic it is, then, in this day of neuroses, of nervous breakdowns, of tranquilizing pills, of mental distress.

Now the apostle gives a closing bit of advice concerning the **4:8** thought life. The Bible everywhere teaches that we can control what we think. It is useless to adopt a defeatist attitude, saying that we simply cannot help it when our minds are filled with unwelcome thoughts. The fact of the matter is that we *can* help it. The secret lies in positive thinking. It is what is now a well-known principle—the expulsive power of a new affection. A person cannot entertain evil thoughts and thoughts about the Lord Jesus at the same time. If, then, an evil thought should come to him, he should immediately get rid of it by meditating upon the Person and Work of Christ. The more enlightened psychologists and psychiatrists of the day have come to agree with the apostle Paul in this matter. They stress the dangers of negative thinking.

You do not have to look very closely to find the Lord Jesus Christ in verse 8. Everything that is true, honest, just, pure, lovely, of good report, virtuous, and praiseworthy is found in Him. Let us look at these virtues one by one: *True* means not false or unreliable, but genuine and real. *Honest* means honorable or morally attractive. *Just* means righteous, both toward God and man. *Pure* would refer to the high moral character of a person's life. *Lovely* has the idea of that which is admirable or fair to behold or to consider. *Of good report* has also been translated "of good repute" or "fair sounding." *Virtue,* of course, speaks of moral excellence, and *praise* means more literally, praiseworthy, something that deserves to be commended.

In verse 7, Paul had assured the saints that God would garrison their hearts and thoughts in Christ Jesus. But he is not neglectful to remind them that they, too, have a responsibility in the matter. God does not garrison the thought-life of a man who does not want it to be kept pure.

Again the apostle Paul sets himself forth as a pattern saint. He **4:9** urges the believers to practice the things which they learned from him and which they saw in his life.

The fact that this verse comes so closely after verse 8 is significant. Right living results from right thinking. If a person's thought-life is pure, then his life will be pure. On the other hand, if a person's mind is a fountain of corruption, then you can be sure that the stream that issues from it will be filthy also. And we should always remember that if a person thinks an evil thought long enough, he will eventually do it.

Those who are faithful in following the example of the apostle are promised that the God of peace will be with them. In verse 7, the peace of God is the portion of those who are prayerful; here the God of peace is the Companion of those who are holy. The thought here is that God will make Himself very near and dear in present experience to all whose lives are embodiments of the truth.

THANK YOU! (4:10-20)

4:10   In verses 10 through 19, Paul is speaking of the relationship which existed between the church at Philippi and himself in connection with financial assistance. How meaningful these verses have been for saints of God who have been called upon to go through times of financial pressure and reverses!

Paul rejoices that now again, after a period of time had elapsed, the Philippians had sent him practical assistance in the work of the Lord. He does not blame them for the period of time in which no such help was received; he gives them credit that they wanted to send gifts to him but that they did not have the opportunity to do so. "For what you lacked was never the care but the chance of showing it"—Moffatt.

4:11   In handling the whole subject of finances, it is lovely to see the delicacy and courtesy which Paul employs. He does not want them to think that he is complaining about any shortage of funds. Rather, he would have them know that he is quite independent of such mundane circumstances. He had learned to be content, no matter what his financial condition might be. Contentment is really greater than riches, for "if contentment does not produce riches, it achieves the same

5 4

object by banishing the desire for them." "It is a blessed secret when the believer learns how to carry a high head with an empty stomach, an upright look with an empty pocket, a happy heart with an unpaid salary, joy in God when men are faithless"—Selected.

Paul knew how to be abased, that is, by not having the bare **4:12** necessities of life; and he also knew how to abound, that is, by having more given to him at any particular time than his immediate needs required. "Every where and in all things I am instructed both to be full and to be hungry, both to abound and to suffer need." How had the apostle Paul learned such a lesson? Simply in this way: he was confident that he was in the will of God. He knew that wherever he was, or in whatever circumstances he found himself, he was there by divine appointment. If he was hungry, it was because God wanted him to be hungry. If he was full, it was because his Lord had so planned it. Busily and faithfully engaged in the service of his King, he could say, "Even so, Father, for so it seemed good in thy sight."

Then the apostle adds the words which have been a puzzle to **4:13** many. "I can do all things through Christ which strengtheneth me." Could he possibly mean this literally? Did the apostle really believe that there was nothing he could not do? The answer is this: When the apostle Paul said that he could do all things, he obviously meant all things which were God's will for him to do. He had learned that the Lord's commands are the Lord's enablements. He knew that God would never call upon him to accomplish some task without giving the necessary grace. The "all things" of this verse probably apply not so much to great feats of daring as to great privations and hungerings.

In spite of what he had said, he wants the Philippians to know **4:14** that they did well in having fellowship with his affliction. To have fellowship with his affliction probably meant to send money to him to supply his needs during his imprisonment. The fact of the matter is **4:15** that in the past, the Philippians had excelled in the grace of giving. During the early days of Paul's gospel ministry, when he departed from Macedonia, no church had fellowship with him financially except the Philippians.

It is remarkable how these seemingly-unimportant details are **4:16** recorded forever in God's precious Word. This teaches us that what is

55

given to the Lord's servants is given to the Lord. He is interested in every cent. He records all that is done as unto Him, and He rewards with good measure, pressed   down , shaken together, and running over. Even when he was in Thessalonica, they sent once and again unto his need. It is apparent that the Philippians were living so close to the Lord that He was able to direct them in their giving. The Holy Spirit placed a burden upon their hearts for the apostle Paul. They responded by sending money to him once and again, that is, twice. When we remember that Paul was in Thessalonica only two or three weeks, it makes their care for him there all the more remarkable.

4:17   The utter unselfishness of Paul is indicated in this verse. "He was more elated by their gain than by their gift." Greater than his desire for financial help was his longing that fruit should abound to the account of the believers. This is exactly what happens when money is given to the Lord. It is all recorded in the account books and will be repaid a hundredfold in a coming day.

All that we have belongs to the Lord, and when we give to Him, we are only giving Him what is His own. Christians who argue as to whether or not they should tithe their money have missed the point. A tithe or tenth part was commanded to Israelites under the law as the minimum gift. In this age of grace, the question should not be how much shall I give to the Lord, but rather how much dare I keep for myself. It should be the Christian's desire to live economically and sacrificially in order to give an ever-increasing portion of his income to the work of the Lord that men might not perish for want of hearing the gospel of Christ.

4:18   When Paul says "I have all," he means, "I have all I need, and abound." It seems strange in this day of twentieth-century commercialism to hear a servant of the Lord who is not begging for money, but who, on the contrary, admits having sufficient. The unrestrained begging campaigns of the present day are an abomination in the sight of God and a reproach to the Name of Christ. They are completely unnecessary. Hudson Taylor once said, "God's work carried on in God's way will never lack God's resources." The trouble today is that we have failed to distinguish between working for God and the work of God. It is possible to engage in so-called Christian service which might not be the will of God at all. Where there is an abundance of money, there is always the greatest danger of embarking on ventures which might not have the divine sanction. To quote Hudson Taylor once again: "What we greatly need to fear is not insufficient funds, but too much unconsecrated funds."

The gift which Epaphroditus brought from the Philippians to Paul is described as an odor of a *sweet smell*, a *sacrifice* acceptable, well-pleasing to God. The only other time these words are used, they refer to Christ Himself (Ephesians 5:2). Paul dignifies the sacrificial giving of the Philippians by describing what it meant to God. It ascended as a fragrant sacrifice to Him. It was both acceptable and well-pleasing.

"How vast, then, is the range of an apparently local kindness! We thought we were ministering to a pauper, and in reality we were conversing with the King. We imagined that the fragrance would be shut up in a petty neighborhood, and lo, the sweet aroma steals through the universe. We thought we were dealing only with Paul, and we find that we were ministering to Paul's Savior and Lord"—Jowett.

Now Paul adds what is perhaps the best-known and best-loved 4:19
verse in this entire chapter. We should notice that this promise follows the description of their faithful stewardship. In other words, because they had given of their material resources to the Lord, even to the point where their own livelihood was endangered, the Lord would supply their every need. How easy it is to take this verse out of its context and to use it as a soft pillow for Christians who are squandering their money on themselves with seldom a thought for the work of the Lord! "That's all right. The Lord will supply all your need." While it is true in a general sense that God does supply the needs of His people, this is a specific promise that those who are faithful and devoted in their giving to Christ will never lack.

It has often been remarked that God supplies the needs of His people—not *out of* His riches, but *according to* His riches in glory by Christ Jesus. A common illustration is this: If a millionaire gave a dime to a child, he would be giving *out of* his riches. But if he gave a hundred thousand dollars to some worthy cause, he would be giving *according to* his riches. God's supply is *according to* His riches in glory by Christ Jesus, and nothing could be richer than that.

Williams calls verse 19 a note upon the bank of faith: *"My God*—the name of the Banker. *Shall supply*—the promise to pay. *All your need*—the value of the note. *According to His riches*—the capital of the bank. *By Christ Jesus*—the signature at the foot, without which the note is worthless."

4:20   Thinking of God's abundant provision causes the apostle to break out into praise. This is suited language for every child of God who daily experiences God's gracious care, not only in the supply of material things, but also, as Meyer has pointed out, in providing guidance, help against temptation, and the quickening of languishing devotional life.

CLOSING GREETINGS (4:21-23)

4:21   Thinking of the believers as they are gathered together and listening to the letter which he was writing to them, Paul salutes every saint in Christ Jesus and sends greetings from the brethren who are with him.

4:22   We love this verse for its reference to Caesar's household. Our imaginations are strongly tempted to run riot. Who are the members of Nero's household referred to here? Were they some of the soldiers who had been assigned to watch the apostle Paul, and who had been saved through his ministry? Were they slaves or freed men who worked in the palace? Or might the expression include some of the higher officials of the Roman government at that time? We cannot know with certainty, but here we have a lovely illustration of the truth that Christians, like spiders, find their way into kings' palaces. The gospel knows no boundaries. It can penetrate behind the most forbidding walls. It can plant itself in the very midst of those who are seeking to exterminate it. Truly, the gates of hades shall not prevail against the church of Jesus Christ.

4:23   Now Paul closes with this characteristic greeting. Grace sparkled on the first page of this letter, and now it is found again at the close. Out of the abundance of a man's heart his mouth speaks. Paul's heart was filled to overflowing with the greatest theme of all the ages—the grace of God—and it is not at all surprising that this precious truth should flood over into every channel of his life.

Jowett calls this epistle "a little volume of graciousness, bound within the covers of grace." Dr. David Smith says it is "the tenderest thing that Paul ever wrote."

"The greatest of humans has written the warmest of his letters. The love task is finished. It is nightfall. And tomorrow morning, leaving behind the man who still has a chain on his wrist and a soldier by his side, Epaphroditus will be seen striding out toward Philippi, with this under his tunic"—Dr. Paul Rees.

When you are ready, complete Exam 2 by answering questions 11-20 on pages **63-66.** (You should have already answered questions 1-10 as part of your study of lesson 3.)

PHILIPPIANS, COLOSSIANS and PHILEMON   *Exam 2*
                                              Lessons 3, 4

Exam
Grade_____

Name_____
                 (print plainly)

Address _____

                                  Zip   Class
City _____ State _____ Code _____ Number _____

Instructor _____

LESSON 3

In the blank space in the right-hand margin write the letter of the correct answer.
(40 points)

1. When Paul told the Philippians to "rejoice in the Lord," he
    a. recognized that circumstances often make such rejoicing
       impossible
    b. was implying that the loss of joy in the Christian life is
       proof of the loss of salvation
    c. was himself living in happy and congenial circumstances
    d. knew from personal experience that such an attitude was
       possible at all times   _____

2. Paul wanted the Philippians to beware of
    a. speaking in tongues
    b. Judaistic teachers
    c. becoming lukewarm towards the Lord
    d. backslidden Christians   _____

3. **What did Paul consider of great value? His**
    a. former religion
    b. family heritage
    c. personal attainments
    d. knowledge of Christ as Lord and Savior   _____

4. Paul wanted to be
    a. the chiefest of all the apostles
    b. the greatest in the kingdom of God
    c. a martyr for Christ's sake
    d. a second Adam to the human race   _____

5. The textbook takes the expression "if by any means I might attain unto the resurrection of the dead" to mean that
a. there will be a partial rapture of the Church and Paul wanted to be numbered amongst those who would be raised
b. only overcomers will have a share in the first resurrection
c. Paul strongly desired to experience the resurrection and did not care what trials lay between
d. a spiritual truth is in view here, namely that Christians should live victoriously on "resurrection ground"   _____

6. Paul was content with
   a. his spiritual attainments
   b. his material possessions
   c. his success as Christ's servant
   d. his privileges and advantages as a Jew or his natural heritage   _____

7. In depicting to the Philippians his own spiritual goals, Paul employs a figure of himself as a
a. pupil in a school
b. king enthroned in power
c. runner in a race
d. sower planting precious seed   _____

8. Moffatt renders the expression "our conversation is in heaven" as
a. "our citizenship is in heaven"
b. "our civil rights are in heaven"
c. "we are citizens of Glory"
d. "we are a colony of heaven"   _____

9. Under each of the following, list the appropriate items which make up "the whole stock-in-trade of the self-righteous Pharisee." *(6 points)*

a. Pride of Ancestry

   (1) _____

   (2) _____

   (3) _____

   (4) _____

b. Pride of Orthodoxy

_____

c. Pride of Activity

_____

d. Pride of Morality

_____

10. Paul listed four things he coveted in what has been called "the soul's quest for personal Christ." These four things were: *(4 points)*

a. _____

_____

b. _____

_____

c. _____

_____

d. _____

_____

LESSON 4

n the blank space in the right-hand margin write the letter of the correct answer.
'40 points)

11. One of the secrets of Paul's success in the work of the Lord, as
revealed in his letter to the Philippians, was his
a. scholarship and great learning
b. genuine love for people
c. eloquence and gifted oratory
d. influence with men in high positions of authority   _____

12. Euodias and Syntyche were
 a. two of Paul's natural sisters who had left the ancestral home of Tarsus to settle in Philippi
 b. elders in the Philippian church
 c. sisters in the local church at Philippi who were squabbling
 d. two of Paul's many "mothers" in Christ who had been hospitable to him and given him much encouragement

_____

13. According to this lesson, Paul's "true yoke-fellow" was
 a. Timothy
 b. Luke
 c. Epaphroditus
 d. Clement

_____

14. Which of the following is *NOT* envisioned as a woman's sphere of service in the expression "they labored with me in the gospel"?
 a. preaching the gospel in public
 b. extending hospitality
 c. home visitation
 d. teaching children
 e. personal witness

_____

15. The expression "be careful for nothing"
 a. means that the Christian should be anxious about nothing
 b. is typical Pauline hyperbole
 c. is missing from the original text
 d. is qualified by other Scriptures, and rightly so since, as it stands, the words present an impossible standard

_____

16. Paul thanked the Philippians for
 a. appealing his case to the supreme court at Rome
 b. sending him financial aid
 c. inviting him to come back to Philippi for a series of special evangelistic meetings
 d. speaking well of him even though his name and reputation were being slandered by his enemies

_____

17. Paul's testimony was—
 a. "I have never been in want"
 b. "There's absolutely nothing I cannot do"
 c. "Come what may, I am content"
 d. "I came, I saw, I conquered"

_____

18. Christian giving should be
   a. regulated by the Old Testament law of the tithe
   b. sacrificial in character and increasing in amount
   c. motivated by the hope of getting back more than is given
      by a God Who is "no man's debtor"
   d. done openly and publicly with a view to human praise
   e. governed by the amount of tax-deduction allowed _____

19. Paul lists a number of things which should positively occupy the thinking of the child of God. List five of these and give a brief definition for each. *(5 points)*

   a. _____ _____

   _____

   b. _____ _____

   _____

   c. _____ _____

   _____

   d. _____ _____

   _____

   e. _____ _____

   _____

20. Write out from memory Philippians 4:19. *(5 points)*

   _____

   _____

   _____

   _____

   _____

WHAT DO YOU SAY?

State one principle about giving which has impressed you.

_____

_____

For You I Am Praying

Colossians 1:1-14

I. Salutation (vv. 1, 2).

II. Paul's thanksgiving for what he had heard of the faith, love and hope of the Colossian Christians (vv. 3-8).

III. The Apostle's prayer that the saints might:
   a. be filled with the full knowledge of God's will (v. 9).
   b. walk worthy of the Lord (v. 10).
   c. be strengthened with all power (v. 11).
   d. be thankful for what God had done for them (vv. 12-14).

INTRODUCTION

Colosse was a city in the province of Phrygia, in the area which we now know as Asia Minor. If you will look on a Bible map, you will see that it was located close to the cities of Hierapolis and Laodicea, mentioned in chapter 4:13. In fact, it was ten miles east of Laodicea and thirteen miles south-east of Hierapolis. It was also located about 100 miles east of Ephesus, at the mouth of a pass in the Cadmian range (a narrow glen 12 miles long—Ramsay), on the military route from the Euphrates to the West. Originally Colosse was larger than at the time of its mention in the Bible. The name is thought possibly to relate to the word "colossus," from the fantastic shapes of limestone formations. Colosse was on the Lycus (Wolf) river, which flows westward into the Maeander shortly after it passes Laodicea, where the water from the hot springs of Hierapolis joins the cold waters from Colosse, producing a "luke-warm" condition at Laodicea. Hierapolis was both a health center and a religious center, while Laodicea was the metropolis of the valley. At the time this Epistle was written, Colosse was the smallest of the three. Bishop Lightfoot says, "Without doubt Colosse was the least important church to which any Epistle of St. Paul was addressed." Its glory had long since departed, and while Laodicea and Hierapolis have a large place in the early records of the Christian Church, Colosse soon disappeared. (See *Cambridge Bible* and *New Bible Commentary*.)

We do not have exact information as to how the gospel first reached this city. At the time when Paul wrote this letter, he had never met the believers in Colosse (2:1). It is generally believed that Epaphras (pronounced EP-a-fras) was the one who first brought the good news of salvation to this city (1:7). Many believe that Epaphras may have been converted through Paul when he spent the three years at Ephesus. Phrygia is a part of Proconsular Asia, and Paul was in Phrygia (Acts 16:6; 18:23), but not Colosse (2:1).

As to the time and place when this epistle was written, there is considerable disagreement. Perhaps most Bible teachers feel that Paul wrote the letter from Rome while he was a prisoner there, A.D. 61-62 (Acts 28:30, 31). He might have met Epaphras in Rome while they were both imprisoned for the cause of the gospel. In all fairness, however, it should be said that many feel the letter was written from Caesarea, during Paul's imprisonment there (Acts 23:25; 24:27). Others believe that it was written from Ephesus. Fortunately for us, an understanding of the epistle does not depend on a full knowledge of the circumstances under which it was written.

We do know from the letter that a false teaching known as Gnosticism was threatening the church at Colosse. The Gnostics prided themselves on their knowledge. They claimed to have information superior to that of the apostles. They tried to create the impression that a person could not be truly happy unless he had been initiated into the deeper secrets of their cult.

Some of the Gnostics denied the true humanity of Christ. They taught that the Christ was a divine influence that came out from God and rested upon the man, Jesus, at His baptism. They further taught that the Christ left Jesus in the Garden of Gethsemane, just before His crucifixion. The result was that Jesus died, but the Christ did not die, according to them.

Certain branches of Gnosticism taught that between God and matter there were various levels or grades of spirit beings. They adopted this view in an effort to explain the origin of evil. "The Gnostic speculation concerned itself primarily with the origin of the universe and the existence of evil. They assume that God is good and yet there is evil in existence. Their theory was that evil is inherent in matter. And yet the good God could not create evil matter. So they postulated a series of Emanations, aeons, spirits, angels that came in between God and matter. The idea was that one aeon came from God, another aeon from this aeon, and so on till there was one far enough away from God for God not to be contaminated by the creation of evil matter and yet close enough to have power to do the work"—A. T. Robertson.

Believing that the body was inherently sinful, the Gnostics practiced asceticism, a system of self-torture or self-denial, in an effort to attain a higher spiritual state.

It seems that traces of two other errors were found in Colosse. These were antinomianism and Judaism. Antinomianism is the teaching that a person under grace needs not practice self-control but may give full satisfaction to his bodily appetites and passions. Judaism had become a system of ceremonial observances by which a man hoped to achieve righteousness before God.

All the errors which existed in the days of the church at Colosse are still with us today. Gnosticism has reappeared in Christian Science, Theosophy, Jehovah's Witnesses, Unity, and other systems. Antinomianism is characteristic of all who say that because we are under grace, we can live as we please. Judaism was originally a God-given revelation, whose forms and ceremonies were intended to teach spiritual truths in a typical way, as the Epistle to the Hebrews and other portions of the New Testament show. This lapsed into a system in which the forms themselves were considered to be meritorious, and so the spiritual meaning was often largely ignored. It has its counterpart today in the many religious systems which teach that man may gain merit and favor with God by his own works, ignoring or denying his sinful state, and need of salvation from God alone.

In this epistle, we shall see how the apostle Paul deals masterfully with all these errors by setting forth the glories of the Person and Work of the Lord Jesus Christ.

It should be mentioned that this epistle bears a striking resemblance to Paul's letter to the Ephesians. However, it is a resemblance without repetition. Ephesians views believers as seated with Christ in heavenly places. Colossians, on the other hand, sees believers on earth, with Christ their glorified Head in heaven. The emphasis in Ephesians is that the believer is in Christ. Colossians speaks of Christ in the believer, the hope of glory. In the Epistle to the Ephesians, the emphasis is on the church as the "body" of Christ, "the fulness of him that filleth all in all" (Ephesians 1:23). Hence the unity of the body of Christ is stressed. In Colossians, the Headship of Christ is set forth extensively in chapter 1, with the necessity of our "holding fast the head" (2:18, 19), being submissive to Him. Fifty-four of the one hundred and fifty-five verses in Ephesians are similar to verses which are found in Paul's letter to the Colossians.

SALUTATION (1:1-2)

1:1 In the days when the New Testament was written, it was customary to begin a letter with the name of the writer. Thus Paul introduces himself as "an apostle of Christ Jesus through the will of God" (A.S.V.). An apostle was one who had been especially sent forth by the Lord Jesus as a messenger. In order to confirm the message that they preached, apostles were given the power to perform miracles (2 Corinthians 12: 12). In addition, we read that when the apostles laid their hands on believers in certain cases, the Holy Spirit was given (Acts 8:15-20; 19:6). There are no apostles in the world today in the strict sense of the word, and it is folly for men to claim to be successors of the original twelve. Ephesians 2:20 is taken by some to indicate that the work of those with the distinctive gift of apostles and prophets had to do chiefly with the founding of the church, in contrast with the work of evangelists, pastors, and teachers (Ephesians 4:11), which continue throughout this dispensation.

Paul traces his apostleship to the will of God (see also Acts 9:15; Galatians 1:1). It was not an occupation which he had chosen for himself or for which he had been trained by men. Neither was the office given to him by human ordination. It was not "of men" (as the source), neither "by man" (as the instrument). Rather, his entire ministry was carried out under the solemn realization that God Himself had chosen him to be an apostle.

With Paul at the time this letter was written was "Timothy our brother." It is nice to notice here complete lack of officialism in Paul's attitude toward Timothy. Both were members of a common brotherhood and there was no thought of a hierarchy of church dignitaries with pompous titles and distinguishing clothing.

The letter is addressed to "the saints and faithful brethren in **1:2** Christ which are at Colosse." Here are two of the lovely names that are given in the New Testament to all Christians. "Saints" means that they are separated to God from the world and that as a result they should lead holy lives. "Faithful brethren" indicates that they are children of a common Father through faith in the Lord Jesus; they are believing brethren. Christians are also called disciples and believers in other sections of the New Testament.

"In Christ" speaks of their spiritual position. When they were saved, God placed them in Christ, "accepted in the beloved." Henceforth, they had His life and nature. Henceforth, they would no longer be seen by God as children of Adam or as unregenerate men, but He would now see them in all the acceptability of His own Son. The expression "in Christ" conveys more of intimacy, acceptance, and security than any human mind can understand. The geographical location of these believers is indicated by the expression "which are at Colosse." It is doubtful that you or I would ever have heard of this city had it not been that the gospel was preached there and souls were saved.

Paul now greets the saints with the lovely salutation, "Grace be unto you and peace, from God our Father and the Lord Jesus Christ." No two words could better embrace the blessings of Christianity than

71

"grace and peace." "Grace" was the common Greek greeting, while "peace" was the common Jewish greeting; and the words were used at meeting or parting. Paul united them, and elevated their meaning and use. Grace pictures God stooping down to sinful, lost humanity in loving and tender compassion. Peace summarizes all that results in the life of a person when he accepts God's grace as a free gift. "Grace can mean many things, and is like a blank check. Peace is definitely part of the Christian's heritage, and we should not allow Satan to rob us of it"—R. J. Little. The order of the words is significant: grace first, then peace. If God had not first acted in love and mercy toward us, we would still be in our sins. But because He took the initiative and sent His Son to die for us, we now can have peace with God, peace with man, and the peace of God in our souls. Having said all this, we should just add that one despairs of ever adequately defining such tremendous words as these.

THANKSGIVING (1:3-8)

1:3 Having greeted these saints in terms which have become the watchword of Christianity, the apostle does something else which is very characteristic of him—he falls to his knees in thanksgiving and prayer. It seems that the apostle always began his prayer with praise to the Lord, and this would be a good example for us to follow also. His prayer is addressed to "God and the Father of our Lord Jesus Christ." Prayer is the unspeakable privilege of having audience with the Sovereign of the universe. But it may be asked, "How could a mere man dare to stand in the awful presence of the infinitely high God?" The answer is found in our text. The glorious and majestic God of the universe is the Father of our Lord Jesus Christ. The One who is infinitely high has become intimately nigh. Because as believers in Christ we share His life, God is our Father also (John 20:17). We can draw near through Christ. "Praying always for you." Taken by itself, this expression does not seem remarkable, but it takes on new meaning when we remember that this describes Paul's interest in people whom he had never met. We often find it difficult to remember our own relatives and friends before the throne of grace, but think of the prayer list the apostle Paul must have kept! He prayed not only for those whom he knew but also for the Christians in faraway places whose names had been mentioned to him by others. Truly Paul's untiring prayer life helps us to understand him better.

What had he heard about these Colossians? He had heard of their 1:4 faith in Christ Jesus and of their love to all the saints. Notice that he first mentions their faith in Christ Jesus. That is where we must always begin. There are many religious people in the world today who are constantly talking about their love for others. But if you question them, you find that they do not have any faith in the Lord Jesus. Such love is then hollow and meaningless. On the other hand, there are those who profess to have faith in Christ, yet you look in vain for any evidence of love in their lives. Paul would likewise question the sincerity of their faith. There must be true faith in the Savior, and this faith must be evidenced by a life of love to God and to one's fellow man.

Paul speaks of faith as being in Christ Jesus. It is very important to notice this. The Lord Jesus Christ is always set forth in Scripture as the Object of faith. A person might have unbounded faith in a bank, but that faith is only valid as long as the bank is reliable. The faith itself will not insure the safety of one's money if the bank is poorly managed. So it is in spiritual life. Faith in itself is not sufficient. That faith must be centered in the Lord Jesus Christ. Since He can never fail, no one who trusts Him will ever be disappointed.

The fact that Paul had heard of their faith and of their love shows that they certainly were not secret believers. In fact, the New Testament gives little encouragement to anyone who seeks to go on as a secret disciple. The teaching of the Word of God is that if a person has truly received the Savior, then it is inevitable that he will make public confession of Christ.

Notice that the love of the Colossians went out to *all* the saints. There was nothing local or sectarian about their love. They did not love only those of their own fellowship, but wherever they found those who were true believers, their love flowed out freely and warmly. This should be a lesson to us that our love should not be narrow, should not be limited to our own local fellowship, or to missionaries from our own country. We should recognize the sheep of Christ wherever they are found, and manifest our affection to them wherever possible.

1:5   It is not entirely clear how this verse connects with what has gone before. Is it connected with verse three: "We give thanks . . . for the hope which is laid up for you in heaven"? Or is it connected with the latter part of verse four: "The love which ye have to all the saints, because of the hope which is laid up for you in the heavens" (A.S.V.)? Either interpretation is possible. The apostle could be giving thanks, not only for their faith and their love, but also for the future inheritance which would one day be theirs. On the other hand, it is also true that faith in Christ Jesus and love to all the saints are exercised in view of that which lies before us. " 'The hope' is not here 'so much the act of hoping, as the object hoped for' " (C. H. Dodd). In any case, we can all see that Paul is here listing the three cardinal virtues of the Christian life: faith, love, and hope. These are also mentioned in 1 Corinthians 13:13 and 1 Thessalonians 1:3; 5:8. "Faith rests on the past; love works in the present; hope looks to the future"—Lightfoot.

In this verse, the word "hope" does not mean the attitude of waiting or looking forward to something, but rather it refers to that for which a person hopes. Here it means the fulfillment of our salvation when we shall be taken to heaven and will enter into our eternal inheritance. The Colossians had heard about this hope previously, perhaps when Epaphras preached the gospel to them. What they had heard is described as the "word of the truth of the gospel." The gospel is here described as a message of *true* glad tidings. Perhaps Paul was thinking of the *false* teachings of the Gnostics when he wrote this. Someone has defined "truth" as that which God says about a thing (John 17:17). The gospel is true because it is God's Word.

1:6   The truth of the gospel had come to the Colossians even as it had to all the then-known world. This must not be taken in an absolute sense. It does not mean that *every man and woman* in the world had heard the gospel. It may mean, in part that some from *every nation* had heard the good news of salvation (Acts 2). It may also mean that the gospel was for all men, and was being spread abroad without purposeful limitation. Paul is also describing the inevitable results which it produced. The American Standard Version conveys this thought: "Which is come unto you; even as it is also in all the world, bearing fruit and increasing." In other words, in Colosse and in all the other parts of the world where the gospel was preached, it bore fruit and increased. This is stated to show the supernatural character of the gospel. In nature, a plant does not usually bear fruit and increase at the same time. Many times, it has to be pruned in order to bear fruit, for if it is allowed to grow wild, the result is that all the life of the plant goes into leaves and branches rather than into fruit. But the gospel does both at the same time. It bears fruit in the salvation of souls and in the upbuilding of the saints, and it also spreads from city to city and from nation to nation.

This is precisely the effect that the gospel had in the lives of the Colossians since the day they heard and knew the grace of God in truth. There was numerical growth in the church at Colosse and, in addition, there was spiritual growth in the lives of the believers there.

Although verse 6 does not refer to the extent of the spread of the gospel up to that time, it appears that great strides had been made in the first century, and that the gospel did reach into Europe, Asia, and Africa, going farther than many persons have supposed. Still, there is no ground for thinking that it covered the entire earth. "The grace of God" is used here as a lovely description of the gospel message. What could more beautifully summarize the glad tidings than the wonderful truth of God's grace bestowed on guilty men!

The apostle clearly states that it was from Epaphras that the 1:7 believers had heard the gospel message and had come to know it experentially in their lives. Paul commends Epaphras as a beloved fellow-servant and a faithful minister of Christ. There was nothing of bitterness or jealousy about the apostle Paul. It did not bother him to see another preacher receiving commendation. In fact, he was the first to express his appreciation for other servants of the Lord. In the King James Version, the last clause of this verse reads, "who is for you a faithful minister of Christ." However, it is now generally agreed that the correct translation is, "who is a faithful minister of Christ on our (or my) behalf."

It was from Epaphras that Paul himself had heard of the Colos- 1:8 sians' love in the Spirit. This was not a merely human affection, but it was that genuine love for the Lord and for His people which is created by the indwelling Holy Spirit of God. This, incidentally, is the only reference to the Holy Spirit in this epistle.

PRAYER (1:9-14)

1:9 Having concluded this thanksgiving, the apostle Paul now begins to make specific intercession for the saints. We have already mentioned how broad were the apostle's prayer interest. We should further point out here that his requests were always specifically suited to the needs of the people of God in any particular location. He did not pray in generalities. Here he seems to make four separate requests for the Colossians: (1) Spiritual insight; (2) A worthy walk; (3) Abundant power; (4) A thankful spirit.

And please notice that there was nothing mean or stingy about his requests. This is especially obvious in verses 9, 10, and 11 by his use of the words *all* and *every*. (1) *All* wisdom and spiritual understanding (v. 9). (2) *All* pleasing (v. 10). (3) *Every* good work (v. 10). (4) *All* might (v. 11). (5) *All* patience and longsuffering (v. 11).

Now back to verse 9. "For this cause" connects with the preceding verses. It means *because of Epaphras' report* (vv. 4, 5, 8). From the first time he had heard about these dear saints at Colosse and their faith, love, and hope, the apostle had made it his practice to pray for them. First, he prayed that they might be filled with the knowledge of God's will in all spiritual wisdom and understanding (A.S.V.). He did not ask that they should be satisfied with the boasted knowledge of the Gnostics. He would have them enter into the full knowledge of God's will for their lives as revealed in His Word. This knowledge is not of a worldly or carnal nature; it is characterized by spiritual wisdom and understanding—wisdom to apply the knowledge in the best way, and understanding to see what agrees and what conflicts with God's will.

1:10 There is a very important connection between this verse and the preceding one. Why did the apostle Paul want the Colossians to be filled with the knowledge of God's will? Was it that they might become mighty preachers? Or sensational teachers? Was it that they might attract large followings to themselves, as the Gnostics sought to do?

No, the true purpose of spiritual wisdom and understanding is to enable Christians to walk worthy of the Lord unto all pleasing. This does not mean "pleasing all men" but "pleasing God in all things." Here we have a very important lesson on the subject of guidance. God does not reveal His will to us in order to satisfy our curiosity. Neither is it intended to cater to our ambition or pride. Rather the Lord shows us His will for our lives in order that we might please Him in all that we do.

"Being fruitful in every good work." Here is a helpful reminder that although a person is not saved *by* good works, he most certainly is saved *unto* good works. Sometimes in emphasizing the utter worthlessness of good works in the salvation of souls, we are likely to create the impression that Christians do not believe in good works. Nothing could be farther from the truth. We learn in Ephesians 2:10 that "we are His workmanship, created in Christ Jesus unto good works." Again, Paul wrote to Titus, "This is a faithful saying, and these things I would that thou affirm constantly, that they which have believed in God might be careful to maintain good works" (Titus 3:8).

And not only did the apostle want them to bear fruit in every good work, but also to increase in the knowledge of God. How is this done? First of all, it is done through the diligent study of God's Word. Then it is also found in obeying His teachings and serving Him faithfully. (The latter seems to be the prominent thought here.) As we do these things, we enter into a deeper knowledge of the Lord. "Then shall we know, if we follow on to know the Lord" (Hosea 6:3).

It is interesting to notice the repetition of words dealing with knowledge in Chapter 1 and to realize that there is a definite advance in thought with each use. In verse 6, they *knew* the grace of God." In verse 9, they had "the *knowledge* of His will." In verse 10, they were "increasing in the *knowledge* of God." Perhaps we could say that the first refers to salvation, the second to study of the Scriptures, and the third to service and Christian living. Sound doctrine should lead to right conduct, which expresses itself in obedient service.

The apostle's third request is that the saints might be strengthened **1:11** with all power, according to the might of His glory. (Note the progression: filled, v. 9; fruitful, v. 10; fortified, v. 11.) The Christian life cannot be lived by mere human energy. It requires supernatural strength.

Therefore Paul desires that the believers might know the power of the risen Son of God, and he furthermore desires that they should know this "according to the might of His glory." As has often been pointed out, the request is not that this power might be *out of* the might of His glory but *according to* it. The might of His glory is limitless and that is just the scope of the prayer. "The equipment with power is proportional not simply to the recipient's need, but to the Divine supply"— Peake.

But once again we would ask, "Why did Paul want the Christians to have this power?" Was it that they might go out and perform spectacular miracles? Was it that they might raise the dead, heal the sick, cast out demons? Once again the answer is No. This power is needed so that the child of God may have "all patience and longsuffering with joyfulness." This deserves the student's careful attention. In certain parts of Christendom today, great emphasis is placed upon so-called miracles, such as speaking in tongues, healing the sick, and other similar sensational acts. But there is a greater miracle than all of these in the age in which we live, and that is for a child of God to suffer patiently and to thank God in the midst of his trial.

In 1 Corinthians 13:4, longsuffering is connected with kindness here with joyfulness. We suffer because we cannot escape sharing the groaning of creation. To maintain joyfulness within and kindness to others requires God's power, and is Christian victory. The difference between patience and longsuffering has been defined as the difference between enduring without complaint and enduring without retaliation. God's grace has achieved one of its greatest objects in the life of a believer when he can suffer patiently and praise God in the midst of the fiery trial.

1:12   Who is giving thanks in this verse? Is it the apostle or the Colossians? We believe that it is probably the latter. Paul is praying that they might not only be strengthened with all might but that they also might have a thankful spirit, that they might never fail to express their gratitude to the Father, Who made them "meet to be partakers of the inheritance of the saints in light." As sons of Adam, we were not fit to enjoy the glories of heaven. In fact, if an unsaved man could somehow be taken to heaven, he would not enjoy it, but would rather be in

78

the deepest misery. Appreciation of heaven requires a fitness for it. Even as believers in the Lord Jesus Christ, we do not have any fitness in ourselves for heaven. The only title to glory which we have is found in the Person of the Lord Jesus Christ.

> "I stand upon His merit,
> I know no other stand,
> Not e'en where glory dwelleth,
> In Immanuel's land."

When God saves a person, He instantly bestows on that person fitness for heaven. As we have said before, that fitness is Christ. Nothing can improve on that. Not even a long life of obedience and service here on earth makes a person more fit for heaven than he was the day he was saved. Our title to glory is found in His blood. While the inheritance is "in light" and "reserved in heaven," we believers on earth have the Holy Spirit as the "earnest of our inheritance." Therefore we can rejoice in what lies ahead for us, while enjoying even now the "first-fruits of the Spirit."

In making us "meet to be partakers of the inheritance of the saints in light," God has "delivered us from the power of darkness, and hath translated us into the kingdom of His dear Son." This means that we have been taken out of Satan's domain and placed in the kingdom of the Son of God's love (compare 1 John 2:11). This can be illustrated by the experience of the children of Israel, as recorded in the book of Exodus. They had been living in Egypt, groaning under the lashes of the taskmasters there. By a marvelous act of divine intervention, God delivered them out of that fearful bondage and led them through the wilderness to the promised land. Similarly, as sinners we were in bondage to Satan, but through Christ we have been delivered from his clutches and now we are subjects of Christ's kingdom. Satan's kingdom is one of "darkness"—an absence of light, warmth, and joy; while the kingdom of Christ is one of "love," which implies the presence of all three.

The kingdom of Christ is seen in Scripture in several different aspects. When He came to the earth the first time, He offered a literal

1:13

79

kingdom to the nation of Israel. The Jews wanted deliverance from the Roman oppressor, but they did not want to repent of their sins. Christ could only reign over a people who were in proper spiritual relationship to Him. When that was made clear to them, they rejected their King and crucified Him. Since then, the Lord Jesus has gone back to heaven and we now have the kingdom in mystery form (Matthew 13). This means that the kingdom does not appear in visible form. The King is absent. But all who accept the Lord Jesus Christ during this present age acknowledge Him to be their rightful Ruler, and thus they are subjects of His kingdom. In a coming day, the Lord Jesus will come back to earth, will set up His kingdom with Jerusalem as His headquarters, and will reign for one thousand years. At the end of that time, Christ will put down all enemies under His feet and then He will deliver up the kingdom to God the Father. That will inaugurate the everlasting kingdom, which will continue throughout all eternity.

1:14 Having mentioned the kingdom of God's dear Son, Paul now launches into one of the grandest passages in all the Word of God on the Person and work of the Lord Jesus. It is hard for us to know whether he has finished his prayer, or whether it continues through these verses we are about to study. But it is not of great importance, because even if the following verses are not pure prayer, they certainly are pure worship.

Sturz has pointed out that "in this amazing passage which exalts Jesus Christ more than any other, His name does not appear even once in any form." While this is remarkable in one sense, yet it is not to be wondered at. For who else but our blessed Savior could ever fulfil the description which is given to us here? The passage reminds us of Mary's question to the gardener, "Sir, if thou have borne him hence, tell me where thou hast laid him and I will take him away" (John 20:15). She did not name Him. There was only one Person in her view.

Christ is first presented as the One "in whom we have redemption . . . even the forgiveness of sins." Redemption describes the act whereby we were bought from the slave market of sin. The Lord Jesus, as it were, put a price tag upon us. How highly did He value us? He said, in effect, "I value them so highly that I am willing to shed My blood to purchase them." Since we have been purchased at such a tremendous cost, it should be clear to us that we no longer belong to ourselves; we have been bought with a price. Therefore we should not live our lives the way we choose. Borden of Yale pointed out that if we take our lives and do what we want with them, we are taking something that does not belong to us, and therefore we are thieves!

Not only has He redeemed us; He has given us "the forgiveness of sins." This means that God has cancelled out the debt which our sins incurred. The Lord Jesus Christ paid the penalty on the cross of Calvary; it never needs to be paid again. The account is settled and closed, and God has not only forgiven, but He has removed our sins as far as the east is from the west (Psalm 103:12).

It comes as a shock to many Christians to learn that the expression "through His blood" should not be included in this verse. Even such a dependable translator as J. N. Darby omits it as not being found in the best manuscripts. This does not at all affect the truth that our redemption is through the blood of the Lord Jesus Christ. That truth is clearly stated in Ephesians 1:7 and other Scriptures. Wm. Kelly remarks, "The object evidently is not so much to dwell on the work of Christ as to bring out His personal glory."

When you have mastered this lesson, take the first part of Exam 3 (covering lesson 5), questions 1-10 on pages 93-95 (right after lesson 6).

The Glories of Christ

Colossians 1:15-23

IV. The Glories of Christ (vv. 15-23).

   a. the image of God (v. 15).

   b. the first-born of all creation (v. 15).

   c. the Designer, Creator, Object, and Sustainer of the universe (vv. 16, 17).

   d. the Head of the church (v. 18).

   e. the firstborn from the dead (v. 18).

   f. the pre-eminent One (v. 18).

   g. the possessor of all fulness (v. 19).

   h. the reconciler of all things (vv. 20-23).

THE LORD OF ALL (1:15-19)

In the next four verses, we have the Lord Jesus described (1) in His relationship to God (v. 15); (2) in His relationship to creation (vv. 16, 17); (3) in His relationship to the church (v. 18). **1:15**

The Lord Jesus is here described as the image of the invisible God. The word "image" carries with it at least two ideas. First of all, it conveys to our mind the thought that the Lord Jesus has enabled us to see what God is like. God is Spirit and is therefore invisible. But in the Person of the Lord Jesus Christ, God made Himself visible to mortal eyes. In that sense the Lord Jesus is the image of the invisible God.

83

"Whoever has seen Him has seen the Father" (John 14:9). But the word "image" also conveys the idea of "representative." God had originally placed Adam on the earth to represent His interests, but Adam failed. Therefore, God sent His only Son into the world as His representative to care for His interest and to reveal His heart of love to man. In that sense, He is the image of God. The same word "image" is used in 3:10, where believers are said to be the image of Christ.

Christ is also "the firstborn of every creature," or "of all creation," or "of every created being." What does this mean? Some false teachers today would suggest that the Lord Jesus is Himself a created being. They say that He was the first person whom God ever made. Some of them are even willing to go so far as to admit that He is the greatest creature ever to come from the hand of God. But nothing could be more directly contrary to the teaching of the Word of God than such a thought.

Actually the expression "firstborn" has at least three different meanings in Scripture. In Luke 2:7, it is used in a literal sense, where Mary brought forth her firstborn son. There it means that the Lord Jesus was the first Child to Whom she had ever given birth. In Exodus 4:22, on the other hand, it is used in a figurative sense. "Israel is my son, even my firstborn." In that verse there is no thought of an actual birth having taken place, but the Lord is using this word to describe the distinctive place which the nation of Israel had in His plans and purposes. Finally, in Psalm 89:27, the word "firstborn" is used to designate a place of superiority, of supremacy, of uniqueness. There God says that He will make David His firstborn, higher than the kings of the earth. David was actually the last-born son of Jesse according to the flesh. But God determined to give him a place of unique supremacy, primacy, sovereignty.

Is not that exactly the thought of Colossians 1:15, "the firstborn of every creature"? It means that the Lord Jesus Christ is God's unique Son. In one sense all believers are sons of God, but the Lord Jesus Christ is God's Son in a way that is not true of any other. He existed before all creation and occupies a position of supremacy over it. His is the rank of eminence and dominion. The expression "firstborn of every creature" has nothing to do with birth here. It simply means that He is God's Son by an eternal relationship. It is a title of priority of *position,* and not simply one of time.

As we have mentioned, false teachers have used the previous verse to teach that the Lord Jesus was a created being. Error can usually be refuted from the very passage of Scripture which the cultists use. That is the case here. Verse 16 states conclusively that the Lord Jesus is not a creature, but the very Creator. In this verse we learn that all things—the whole universe of things—were created *in* Him and *through* Him and *unto* Him. Each of these prepositions conveys a different thought. First of all, we read in the A.S.V. "that *in* Him were all things created." Here the thought is that the Lord Jesus had the possibility of creation in Himself. The power to create was in His Being. He was the Architect. Later in the verse we learn that all things have been created *through* Him. This speaks of Him as the active Agent in creation. He was the Person of the Godhead who performed the creative act. Finally, all things were created *unto* Him. He is the One for Whom all things were created, the goal of creation.

The Apostle seems to go to great lengths to emphasize that *all* things were created by Him, whether things in the heavens or things upon the earth. This leaves no loophole for anyone to suggest that although He created some things, He Himself was created originally.

The Apostle then goes on to state that the Lord's creation included things visible and things invisible. The expression "things visible" needs no explanation, but doubtless the Apostle Paul realized that when he said "things invisible" he would arouse our curiosity. Therefore, he proceeds to give a break-down of what he means by "things invisible." They include thrones, dominions, principalities, and powers. Even this is not enough to satisfy our curiosity. But we believe that these terms refer to angelic beings, although we cannot distinguish the different ranks of these intelligent beings.

You will remember that we pointed out in the introduction to this course that the Gnostics thought that there were various ranks and classes of spirit beings between God and matter, and that Christ belonged to one of these classes. In our day the Spiritists claim that Jesus Christ is an advanced spirit in the sixth sphere. Jehovah's Witnesses teach that before our Lord came into the world, he was a created

85

angel and none other than the archangel Michael. Here Paul vigorously
refutes such ideas by stating in the clearest possible terms that the Lord
Jesus Christ is the Creator of angels—in fact, of all beings, whether
visible or invisible.

1:17   "He is before all things, and in Him all things consist" (A.S.V.)
It is interesting to note that Paul says, "He is before all things," not
"He was before all things." The present tense is often used in the Bible
to describe the timelessness of Deity. You will remember that the Lord
Jesus said, for instance, "Before Abraham was, I am."

And not only did the Lord Jesus exist before there was any
creation, but also "by Him all things consist." This means that He is the
Sustainer of the universe and the Source of its perpetual motion. He
controls the stars and the sun and the moon. Even while He was here
on earth He was the One Who was controlling the laws by which our
universe functions in an orderly manner.

1:18   The dominion of the Lord Jesus not only covers the natural
universe, but it also extends to the spiritual realm. "He is the Head of
the body, the Church." All believers in the Lord Jesus during this dispensation are formed into what is known as the body of Christ, or the
Church. Just as a human body is a vehicle by which the person expresses
himself, so the body of Christ is that vehicle which He has on earth by
which He chooses to express Himself to the world. And He is the Head
of that body. The head speaks of guidance, of dictation, of control. He
occupies the place of pre-eminence in the Church.

We read that He is "the beginning" in this verse. We understand
it to mean the beginning of the new creation (see Revelation 3:14), the
source of spiritual life. This is further explained by the use of the
expression "the firstborn from the dead." Here again we must be careful to emphasize that this does not mean that the Lord Jesus was the
first to rise from the dead. There were cases of resurrection in the Old
Testament as well as in the New. But the Lord Jesus was the first to
rise from the dead *to die no more,* and He rose as the Head of a new
creation. His resurrection is unique, and is the pledge that all who trust
in Him will rise also. It proclaims Him as supreme in the spiritual
creation.

"Christ cannot be second anywhere. He is 'first-born of every creature,' because He has created everything (Colossians 1:15, 16). He is also firstborn from the dead in connection with a redeemed and heavenly family. Thus creation and redemption hand the honors of supremacy to Him because of Who He is and of what He has done; 'that in all things He might have the pre-eminence.' He is first everywhere"—Alfred Mace.

The Lord Jesus has thus a double pre-eminence, first in creation, and then in the Church. God has decreed that in *all things* HE might have the pre-eminence. What an answer this is to those who, in Paul's day and in our own day as well, would seek to rob Christ of His deity, and to make of Him only a created being, however exalted!

As we read these words "that in all things He might have the pre-eminence," it is only proper that we should ask ourselves the question, "Does He have the pre-eminence in my life?"

Scholars tell us that the words "the Father" are not found in the manuscripts for this verse. Thus the verse might read, as in the A.S.V., "For it was the good pleasure that in Him should all the fulness dwell." Darby translates it, "For in Him all the fulness of the Godhead was pleased to dwell." The King James Version makes it sound as if at some point in time the Father was pleased to make all fulness dwell in the Son. The real meaning is that the fulness of the Godhead always dwelt in Christ.

"The gnostic teachers held that Christ was a kind of 'halfway house' to God; He was necessary as a link in the chain, but there were other and better links ahead. 'Go on from Him,' these heretics urged, 'and you will reach the fulness.' 'No,' Paul replies, 'Christ Himself is the absolute fulness' "—Daily Notes of the Scripture Union.

All fulness *dwells* in Christ. The word for *dwell* here means to dwell permanently, and not simply to visit temporarily.

THE RECONCILER OF ALL (1:20-23)

In the King James Version, it is difficult to see the connection of verse 20 with what precedes. The American Standard Version shows that verse 19 is connected with verse 20 as follows: "For it was the good pleasure of the Father . . . through Him to reconcile all things unto

Himself, having made peace through the blood of His cross." In other words, it was not only the good pleasure of the Father that all fulness should dwell in Christ (v. 19), but He was also pleased that Christ should reconcile all things unto Himself.

There are two reconciliations mentioned in this chapter: (1) The reconciliation of things (v. 20), and (2) the reconciliation of persons (v. 21). The first is still future, whereas the second is past for all who have believed in Christ.

To reconcile means to restore to a right relationship or standard, or to make peace where formerly there was enmity. The Bible never speaks of God as needing to be reconciled to man, but always of man being reconciled to God. The mind of man's flesh is enmity toward God (Romans 8:7), and because of this, man needs to be reconciled.

When sin entered the world, man became estranged from God. He adopted an attitude of hostility toward God. Therefore, he needed to be reconciled.

But sin affected all creation, and not just the human family.

1. Certain of the angels had sinned sometime in the past. (However, there is no indication in God's Word that these angels will ever be reconciled. They are "reserved in everlasting chains under darkness unto the judgment of the great day," Jude 6.) In Job 4:18, Eliphaz states that God charged His angels with folly.

2. The animal creation was affected by the entrance of sin: "For the earnest expectation of the creature waiteth for the manifestation of the sons of God . . . For the creature was made subject to vanity . . . For we know that the whole creation groaneth and travaileth in pain together until now" (Romans 8:19-22). The fact that animals suffer sickness, pain, and death is evidence that they are not exempt from the curse of sin.

3. The ground was cursed by God after Adam sinned (Genesis 3:17). This is evidenced by weeds, thorns, and thistles.

4. In the book of Job, Bildad tells us that even the stars are not pure in God's sight (Job 25:5), so apparently sin has affected the stellar world.

5.   Then we read in Hebrews 9:23 that things in heaven itself needed to be purified. We do not know all that is meant by this, but perhaps it suggests that heavenly things have been defiled through the presence of Satan, who has access to God as the accuser of the brethren (Job 1:6, 7; Revelation 12:10). Some think this passage refers to the dwelling place of God; others to the stellar heavens. The latter suggests that it is in the stellar spaces that Satan has access to God. In any case, we are all agreed that the throne of God is certainly not defiled by sin.

One of the purposes of the death of the Lord Jesus was to make possible the reconciliation of persons and things to God. In order to do this, He had to remove the cause of enmity and alienation. This He effectively did by settling the sin question to God's entire satisfaction.

The scope of reconciliation is indicated in this chapter, as follows. (1) All who believe on the Lord Jesus Christ are already reconciled to God (v. 21). Although Christ's reconciling work is sufficient for all mankind, it is only effective for those who avail themselves of it. (2) Eventually all "things" will be reconciled, "whether they be things in earth or things in heaven" (v. 20). This would refer to the animal creation, and to inanimate things that have been defiled by sin. However, it does not refer to Satan, to other fallen angels, or to unbelieving men. Their eternal doom is clearly pronounced in the Scriptures.

It is interesting to notice that reconciliation is not said to extend to "things under the earth." There is a difference between reconciliation and subjugation. The latter is described in Philippians 2:10: "That at the Name of Jesus every knee should bow, of things in heaven, and things in earth, *and things under the earth.*" Or, as Darby translates it, "of heavenly and earthly and infernal beings." All created beings, even fallen angels, will eventually be compelled to bow to the Lord Jesus, but this does not mean that they will be reconciled. We emphasize this because Colossians 1:20 has been used to teach the false doctrine of universal salvation, namely, that Satan himself, fallen angels, and unbelieving men will all be reconciled to God eventually. Our passage limits the extent of reconciliation by the phrase "things in earth, or things in heaven." "Things under the earth" are not included.

1:21   Here Paul reminds the Colossians that reconciliation in their case was already an accomplished fact. Before their conversion, the Colossians had been Gentile sinners, alienated from God and at enmity with Him in their minds because of their evil works (Ephesians 4:17, 18, 23). They desperately needed to be reconciled, and the Lord Jesus Christ, in His matchless grace, had taken the initiative.

1:22   He reconciled them in the body of His flesh through death. It was not by His life but by His death. The expression "the body of His flesh" might seem to be strange at first, but doubtless the apostle simply means that the Lord Jesus effected reconciliation by dying on the Cross in a real human body (not as a spirit being, which the Gnostics claimed Him to be). We are here reminded of Hebrews 2:14-16, where Christ's incarnation is declared a necessity in order to effect redemption. The Gnostic concept, of course, denied this.

The wonderful result of this reconciliation is expressed in the words "to present you holy and unblameable and unreproveable in His sight." What a marvelous miracle of grace this is, that ungodly sinners can be delivered from their past evil life and translated into such a realm of blessing!

Well might C. R. Erdman say, "In Christ is found a God who is near, who cares, who hears, who pities and who saves."

The full efficacy of Christ's reconciliation with regard to His people will be seen in a coming day when we are presented to God the Father without sin, without stain, and without any charge against us, and when, as worshippers, we shall gladly acknowledge Christ as the Worthy One (Revelation 5).

1:23   Now the apostle Paul adds one of those "if" passages which have proved very disconcerting to many children of God. On the surface, the verse seems to teach that our continued salvation depends on our continuing in the faith. If this is so, how can this verse be reconciled with other portions of the Word of God, such as John 10:28, 29, which declare that no sheep of Christ's can ever perish?

In seeking to answer this question, we would like to state at the outset that the eternal security of the believer is a blessed truth which is set forth clearly in the pages of the New Testament. However, the Scriptures also teach, as in this verse, that true faith always has the quality of permanence, and that if a man has really been born of God, he will go on faithfully unto the end. Continuance is a proof of reality. There is, of course, always the danger of backsliding, but a Christian falls to rise again (Proverbs 24:16). He does not forsake the faith.

We would also like to say that the Spirit of God has seen fit to put many of these so-called "if" passages in the Word of God in order to challenge all those who profess the Name of Christ as to the reality of their profession. We would not want to say anything that might dull the sharp edge of these passages. As someone has said, "These 'if's' in Scripture look on professing Christians here in the world and they come as healthy tests to the soul."

Pridham comments on these challenging verses as follows: "The reader will find, on a careful study of the Word, that it is the habit of the Spirit to accompany the fullest and most absolute statements of grace by warnings which imply a ruinous failure on the part of some who nominally stand in faith . . . Warnings which grate harshly on the ears of insincere profession are drunk willingly as medicine by the godly soul . . . The aim of all such teaching as we have here is to encourage faith, and condemn, by anticipation, reckless and self-confident professors."

Doubtless with the Gnostics primarily in mind, the apostle is urging the Colossians not to be moved away from the hope that accompanies the gospel, or which the gospel inspires. They should continue in the truth which they heard from Epaphras, grounded and stedfast.

Again Paul speaks of the gospel as having been preached to "every creature which is under heaven." The A.S.V. translates this more accurately "which was preached in all creation under heaven." There is quite a difference here. The gospel goes out to all creation, but it has not as yet reached every creature. Paul is arguing the world-wide proclamation of the gospel as a testimonial to its genuineness. He sees in this the evidence that it is adaptable to the needs of mankind everywhere. The verse certainly does not mean that every person in the world at that time had heard the gospel. It was not a fact accomplished, but a process going on.

In the latter part of verse 23, Paul speaks of himself as a minister of the gospel. At the risk of repetition, we would mention again that the word "minister" in the New Testament means simply a servant. It has nothing of officialism about it. It does not denote a lofty office so much as humble service.

When you are ready, complete Exam 3 by answering questions 11-20 on pages 96-98. (You should have already answered questions 1-10 as part of your study of lesson 5.)

PHILIPPIANS, COLOSSIANS and PHILEMON

Exam 3
Lessons 5, 6

Name_____
              (print plainly)

Exam
Grade_____

Address _____

City_____ State _____ Zip Code _____ Class Number _____

Instructor _____

LESSON 5

In the blank space in the right-hand margin write the letter of the correct answer. (50 points)

1. Which of the following describes the location of Colosse? It was
a. close to Ephesus on the old Roman road from Philippi to Spain
b. ten miles from the Lycus river and ten miles south of Hierapolis
c. a hundred miles east of the Euphrates, deep in the valley of the Lycus
d. ten miles east of Laodicea at the mouth of a pass in the Cadmian range

_____

2. Gnostics, amongst other things, taught that
a. man's chief goal should be to enjoy himself
b. the Christ was an emanation of the deity which rested upon the man Jesus from the time of His baptism until the agony in Gethsemane
c. under grace a person is free to sin as much as he pleases
d. ceremonial observances are vital to achieving righteousness before God

_____

93

3. In comparing Ephesians and Colossians it would be most correct to say that
   a. Ephesians views the believer on earth; Colossians views him in heaven
   b. Ephesians emphasizes the Church as the body of Christ; Colossians emphasizes Christ as the Head of the Church
   c. Ephesians puts the stress on the truth that Christ is in the believer; Colossians puts the stress on the truth that the believer is in Christ
   d. Ephesians anticipates the Lord's second coming as that event relates to the believer; Colossians anticipates the Lord's second coming as that event relates to the world _____

4. The title "saints"
   a. is reserved in the New Testament for brethren who excel in holiness
   b. is used in a correct Biblical way only when applied to men and women who have been canonized by the Church
   c. refers to all believers who are equally set apart by God to lead holy lives
   d. is found only in Paul's epistle to Colossians _____

5. One characteristic of Paul's prayers is that he always
   a. begins them with praise to God
   b. starts with confession of sin and failure
   c. rehearses the cardinal virtues of the faith as a kind of liturgy
   d. concludes with the words, "in the Name of Jesus Christ our Lord, Amen" _____

6. In Paul's day
   a. everybody had heard the gospel
   b. the gospel was being spread abroad but with "purposeful limitation" so far as some nations were concerned
   c. some from every nation had probably heard the gospel
   d. the gospel was bearing fruit at one time and growing in its outreach at another time but, like a natural plant, was not doing both at the same time _____

7. The gospel message had been brought to the Colossians by
   a. Epaphras
   b. Paul himself
   c. an evangelistic team sent out from Jerusalem
   d. direct revelation from God to certain Gentile proselytes to Judaism _____

8. The true purpose of "the knowledge of God's will" is to
   a. make us more efficient teachers
   b. enable us to preach with greater assurance
   c. enable us to translate that knowledge into living pleasing to God
   d. offset pride in Gnostic-type knowledge with pride in genuine knowledge from God _____

9. Which is the greater miracle? To
   a. speak in tongues
   b. heal the sick
   c. suffer patiently, even thankfully
   d. prophesy in the church _____

10. In the passage now being studied, God is said to have put us into
   a. the church of Christ
   b. the kingdom of His dear Son
   c. the family of God
   d. the ark of safety _____

WHAT DO YOU SAY?

What does Colossians 1:14 mean to you personally?

_____

_____

_____

_____

_____

LESSON 6

In the blank space in the right-hand margin write the letter of the correct answer.
(50 points)

11. Which of the following is true of the Lord Jesus according to Colossians 1:15? He is
    a. the heir of all things
    b. the only begotten of the Father
    c. the visible expression of the invisible God
    d. the Messiah of Israel

    _____

12. When the Lord is described by Paul as "the firstborn," the clear implication is that
    a. the Lord Jesus is Himself a created being, the first person God ever made
    b. the Lord Jesus is being referred to as the federal Representative of the nation of Israel
    c. the apostle is referring to Christ's physical birth as the firstborn of Mary
    d. Paul has in mind the Lord's priority of position as God's eternal Son

    _____

13. In Colossians 1, Paul claims that the universe was brought into being
    a. by evolutionary forces
    b. as a result of "a fortuitous concourse of atoms"
    c. through the creatorial power of the Lord Jesus
    d. by an unaided fiat of God the Father

    _____

14. The "invisible things" mentioned by Paul in reference to creation have to do with
    a. angel beings of various rank
    b. the atoms which form the unseen building blocks of the universe
    c. those hidden mysteries of the physical universe not yet discovered by science
    d. the various sources of energy which men can measure but which they cannot see

    _____

15. In the passage now being studied, Paul depicts the timeless deity of the Lord Jesus by
  a. calling Jesus the "father of eternity"
  b. using the present tense of the verb "to be"
  c. saying of the Lord that He is the "same yesterday and today and forever"
  d. referring to Him as "the One Who is and Who was and Who is to come" _____

16. Speaking of Christ as the Head, Paul is referring to His relationship to
  a. the world in an age to come
  b. Israel in her covenant relationship with God
  c. the Church
  d. the new earthly kingdom _____

17. The Lord Jesus is referred to as the "firstborn" in various ways in the New Testament. In Colossians Paul mentions that He is the "firstborn" or supreme
  a. only in creation
  b. in creation and redemption
  c. only in redemption
  d. in His earthly family as Mary's firstborn _____

18. Biblically, reconciliation may be defined as
  a. restoring something or someone to a right relationship
  b. paying the price of purchase
  c. becoming used to a situation and learning to live with it even though it may be unpleasant
  d. imparting new life _____

19. Reconciliation extends to
  a. the heavenly realm only
  b. the earthly realm only
  c. all realms including that of the lost in Hell
  d. both the heavenly and the earthly realms but not the realm of the lost _____

20. What should be our attitude towards the "if" passages of Scripture? We should
   a. take them as solemn warnings that it is possible to be truly saved and then to be lost again
   b. regard them as healthy tests to the soul which divide between those who merely profess to be saved and those who genuinely are saved
   c. accept them as plainly contradictory since it is impossible to reconcile them with passages which teach the eternal security of the believer
   d. look upon them as faulty translations or as scribal interpolations which have crept into the body of the text _____

WHAT DO YOU SAY?

How has this lesson increased your appreciation for the Lord Jesus?

_____

_____

_____

_____

_____

The Ministry and the Mystery

Colossians 1:24—2:7

V. Paul's ministry (1:24-29).
   a. Its atmosphere—suffering (v. 24).
   b. Its twofold subject—the gospel and the church (vv. 24-27).
   c. Its object—to present every man perfect in Christ (v. 28).
   d. Its power—God's mighty power (v. 29).

*   *   *

I. Paul's prayer for the saints (2:1-3).
   a. Encouragement (v. 2).
   b. Love (v. 2).
   c. Full assurance (v. 2).
   d. Acknowledgment of the mystery (v. 2).
II. Warning against delusion and persuasive speech (2:4).
III. Exhortation to stedfastness (2:5-7).

PAUL'S MINISTRY (1:24-29)

The remaining six verses of chapter 1 give us a description of Paul's **1:24** ministry. First of all, it was carried out in an atmosphere of suffering. Writing from prison, Paul can say that he now rejoices in his sufferings for the saints, that is, on their account. As a servant of the Lord Jesus Christ, he was called upon to endure untold hardships, persecutions, and afflictions. These to him were a privilege—the privilege of filling up that which was left behind of the afflictions of Christ. What does the apostle Paul mean by this? First of all, we would point out that this cannot refer to the atoning sufferings of the Lord Jesus Christ on the Cross of Calvary. Those were finished once and for all, and no man could ever share in them. But there is a sense in which the Lord Jesus still suffers. You will remember that when Saul of Tarsus was smitten to the ground on the road to Damascus, he heard a voice from heaven saying, "Saul, Saul, why persecutest thou Me?" Saul had not been consciously persecuting the Lord. He had only been persecuting the Christians. He learned, however, that in persecuting believers, he was persecuting their Savior. The Head in heaven feels the sufferings of His body on earth.

Thus, the apostle Paul looks upon all the suffering that Christians are required to go through for the sake of the Lord Jesus as being part of the sufferings of Christ which still remain. They include suffering for righteousness' sake, suffering for His sake (bearing His reproach), and for the gospel's sake.

But the afflictions of Christ refer not only to sufferings *for* Christ. They also describe *the same kind of* sufferings that the Savior endured when He was here, though far less in degree.

The afflictions endured by the apostle in his flesh were for Christ's body's sake, namely, the Church. The sufferings of unsaved people are, in a sense, purposeless. There is no high dignity attached to them. They are only a foretaste of the pangs of hell to be endured forever. But not so the sufferings of Christians. When they suffer for Christ, Christ in a very real way suffers with them.

1:25   "Whereof I am made a minister." The apostle Paul had already used this expression at the close of verse 23. Now he repeats it here in verse 25. However, the careful student will notice that there is a difference in these two usages. The apostle Paul had a twofold ministry: first, he was commissioned to preach the gospel (v. 23); and secondly, he was sent forth to teach the marvelous mystery of the Church (v. 25). This twofold ministry is also described in Ephesians 3:8, 9: first of all, he was sent to preach among the Gentiles the unsearchable riches of Christ, and then he was called to make all men see what is the administration of the mystery. There is a real lesson in this for every true servant of Christ. We are not expected simply to lead men to Christ by the gospel and then abandon them to get along as best they can. Rather we are expected to direct our evangelistic efforts to the formation of local New Testament churches where the converts can be built up in their most holy faith, including the truth of the church. The Lord wants His babes to be directed to feeding stations where they may be nourished and where they may grow.

Thus in Colossians 1 we have seen (1) Christ's twofold preeminence, (2) Christ's twofold reconciliation and (3) Paul's twofold ministry. Here in verse 25, when Paul says, "Whereof I am made a minister," he is referring to his ministry with regard to the church and not the gospel. This is clear from the expression which follows: "According to the dispensation which is given to me for you." The word "dispensation" may also mean "stewardship." A steward is one who cares for the interests or property of another. Paul was a steward in the sense that the great truth of the Church was entrusted to him in a very special way. While the mystery of the body of Christ was not revealed to him alone, yet he was chosen as the one who would carry this precious truth to the Gentiles. Thus "the dispensation of God" means the stewardship which God had given to Paul in connection with preaching the truth of the New Testament church to the Gentile peoples. It includes the unique position of the Church in its relation to Christ and the dispensations, with its constitution, its distinctive hope and destiny, and the many other truths concerning its life and order which God gave to Paul and the other apostles.

When he says, "which is given to me for you," he is thinking of the Colossians as Gentile believers. The apostle Peter had been sent to preach to the Jewish people, while Paul had been entrusted with a similar mission to the Gentiles.

Now we come to one of the more difficult expressions in this chapter, namely, "to fulfil the Word of God." Exactly what does Paul mean by this? First of all, we know that he does not mean that he completed the Word of God by adding the last book to it. As far as we know, the book of Revelation, written by John, was the last book to be added to the New Testament in point of time. In what sense, then, did Paul fulfil or complete the Word of God?

First of all, to fulfil may mean to declare fully, to make known. Thus, Paul had declared the whole counsel of God. We would suggest secondly that he fulfilled the Word of God doctrinally. The great truth of the mystery forms the capstone of the New Testament revelation. In a very real way, it completes the circle of subjects that are covered in the New Testament. While other books were written later than Paul's, yet they did not contain any great mysteries of the faith that are not found in the writings of the apostle Paul. In a very real sense the revelation concerning the mystery of the Church filled up the Word of God. Nothing that was added later was new truth in the same sense.

1:26   That Paul's fulfilling of the Word of God had to do with the mystery is borne out in this verse. "Even the mystery which has been hid from ages and from generations, but now is made manifest to his saints." In the New Testament sense of the word, a mystery is a truth not hitherto revealed, but now made known to the sons of men through the apostles and prophets of the New Testament. It is a truth that man could never have arrived at by his own intelligence but which God has graciously deigned to make known.

This verse is one of many in the New Testament which teaches that the truth of the Church was not known in the Old Testament period. It had been hid from ages and from generations (Ephesians 3: 2-13; Romans 16:25-27). Thus it is wrong to speak of the Church as having begun with Adam or Abraham. The Church began on the day of Pentecost, and the truth of the Church was revealed by the apostles. The Church in the New Testament is not the same as Israel in the Old. It is something that never existed before.

Israel began with God calling Abraham out from Ur of the Chaldees, giving up the rest of the nations to their sins and idolatry. He made a nation out of Abraham's seed, distinct from all others and separate from them. The Church is the reverse of this, and is a union of believers from all races and nationalities into one body, morally and spiritually separated from all others. That the Church is not the continuation of Israel can be seen from a number of things, one being the figure of the "olive tree" which Paul uses in Romans 11 to show that the nation of Israel retains its identity, though the individual Jew who believes in Christ loses his (Colossians 3:10, 11).

The truth of the mystery may be summarized as follows. (1) The Church is the body of Christ. All true believers are members of the body, and are destined to share Christ's glory forever. (2) The Lord Jesus is the Head of the body, providing its life, nourishment, and direction. (3) Jews have no preference as to admission to the church; neither are Gentiles at any disadvantage. Both Jew and Gentile become members of the body through faith and form one new man (Ephesians 2:15; 3:6). That Gentiles could be saved was not a hidden truth in the Old Testament; but that converted Gentiles would be fellow-members of the body of Christ, to be His companions in glory, and to reign with Him, was a truth never previously known.

The particular aspect of the mystery which Paul is emphasizing in verse 27 is that the Lord Jesus is willing to dwell within the Gentile heart. "Christ in you, the hope of glory." This was spoken to the Colossians, who were Gentiles. "That He should dwell in the heart of a child of Abraham was deemed a marvelous act of condescension, but that He should find a home in the heart of a Gentile was incredible"— F. B. Meyer. And yet that is exactly what was involved in the mystery —"that the Gentiles should be fellowheirs, and of the same body, and partakers of His promise in Christ by the gospel" (Ephesians 3:6). To emphasize the importance of this truth, the apostle speaks of "the riches of the glory of this mystery." He does not just say "this mystery" or "the glory of this mystery," but "the riches of the glory of this mystery." He piles words upon words in order to impress his readers with the fact that this is a glorious truth that deserves their closest attention.

". . . which is Christ in you, the hope of glory." The indwelling Christ is the believers' hope of glory. We have no other title to heaven than the Savior Himself. The fact that He indwells us makes heaven as sure as if we were already there.

The expression "whom we preach" is significant. The "whom," of course, refers back to the Lord Jesus Christ (v. 27). Paul is saying that he preached a Person. He did not spend his time on politics or philosophy, but concentrated on the Lord Jesus Himself, because he realized that Christianity is Christ. "Warning every man, and teaching every man in all wisdom; that we may present every man perfect in

Christ Jesus." Here we have further insight into the ministry of the beloved apostle. It was a man-to-man ministry. He warned the unsaved of the awful wrath to come, and he taught the saints the great truths of the Christian faith.

Then we see the emphasis which he placed on follow-up work. He felt a real sense of responsibility toward those whom he had pointed to the Savior. He was not satisfied to see souls saved and then to pass on. He wanted to present every man perfect in Christ Jesus. Paul pictures himself as a priest offering up sacrifices to God. The sacrifices here are men and women. In what condition does he offer them to the Lord? Are they weak or mere babes in Christ? No, he wants them to be mature, full-grown, adult Christians. He wants them to be well-grounded in the truth. Do we share a similar burden for those whom we have led to Christ?

1:29   "Whereunto I labor to weariness, agonizing according to the state of His being at work in me"—Vincent. It was toward this goal that the apostle labored, as well as all the other apostles. And yet he realized that he was not doing this in his own strength, but "according to His working which worketh in me mightily." In other words, he realized that it was only as he was empowered by the Lord that he was able to serve Him at all. He was conscious of the fact that the Lord was working in him mightily as he went from place to place planting churches and feeding the saints of God.

Verses 28 and 29 are especially helpful in Phillips' translation: "So, naturally, we proclaim Christ. We warn everyone we meet, and we teach everyone we can, all that we know about Him, so that, if possible, we may bring every man up to his full maturity in Christ. This is what I am working at all the time, with all the strength that God gives me."

PAUL'S PRAYER (2:1-3)

2:1   This verse is closely linked with the last two verses of chapter one. There the apostle Paul had been describing his strivings, by teaching and preaching, to present every man perfect in Christ. Here his strivings are of a different nature. Now they are spoken of as conflict in prayer. And here this conflict is in behalf of those whom he had never met. From the first day he had heard of the Colossians, he had prayed for them as well as for those in the neighboring city of Laodicea, and for other Christians whom he had not as yet met. (We read of Laodicea again in Revelation 3:14-19. There it pictures the sad state of the church in the days just prior to the Lord's return. We believe that it describes the condition the whole church is in today.)

Verse 1 is a comfort to those who are never privileged to engage in public, platform ministry. It teaches us that we need not be limited by what we can do in the immediate presence of people. We can serve the Lord in the privacy of our closets on our knees. If we do serve publicly, its effectiveness depends largely on the private devotions before God.

The exact content of Paul's prayer is given in this verse. It is **2:2** somewhat difficult to understand it in the King James Version. In such cases, it is often helpful to refer to other versions of the Scriptures. Moffat, for instance, translates the first part of verse 2 as follows: "May their hearts be encouraged! May they learn the meaning of love! May they have all the wealth of conviction that comes from insight! . . ." Arthur Way's translation is: "I yearn that their hearts may be comforted. I want them to be all knit together in mutual love, that love which is the key to all the treasure of the perfect satisfying of our intellect . . ."

The first part of the prayer is that their hearts might be comforted. Here the word "comforted" does not mean consoled in sorrow, but rather strengthened against peril. The Colossians were not undergoing grief at the moment but they were in danger of the teachings of the Gnostics. Therefore "comforted" here means confirmed or strengthened.

The second part of the prayer is that they might be knit together in love. If the saints went on in happy, loving fellowship with one another, they would present a solid flank against the onslaughts of the foe. Also, if their hearts were warm in love to Christ, He would reveal to them the deeper truths of the Christian faith. It is a well-known principle of Scripture that the Lord reveals His secrets to those who are

105

close to Him. The Apostle John, for instance, was the apostle who leaned on Jesus' bosom, and it was no coincidence that he was also the one to whom the great Revelation of Jesus Christ was given.

Next Paul prayed that they might enter into all the riches of the full assurance of understanding. The more they would enter into an understanding of the Christian faith, the more fully convinced they would be of its truthfulness. The more firmly grounded the Christians were in the faith, the less would be the danger of their being led away by the false teachings of the day.

The expression "full assurance" is used three times in the New Testament. "(1) Hebrews 10:22—full assurance of faith—we rest on God's Word, His testimony to us. (2) Colossians 2:2—full assurance of understanding—we know and are assured. (3) Hebrews 6:11—full assurance of hope—we press on with confidence as to the outcome."

The climax of Paul's prayer is found in the words "to the acknowledgment of the mystery of God, and of the Father, and of Christ." The ancient authorities vary a great deal as to the correct text in this passage. The American Standard Version gives what is perhaps the clearest translation: "That they may know the mystery of God, even Christ."

What does Paul mean when he says "that they may know the mystery of God, even Christ"? He is still referring to the truth of the Church—Christ, the Head of the body, and all believers members of the body. But the particular aspect of the mystery which he has in mind is the headship of Christ. He was anxious that the saints should acknowledge this truth. He knew that if they realized the greatness of their Head, they would not be drawn away by Gnosticism or the other evil cults that threatened them.

Paul wanted the saints to use Christ, to utilize His resources, to draw upon Him in every emergency. He wanted them to see that "Christ, Who is *in* His people, is possessed of every attribute of deity, and of infinite, unutterable, measureless resources, so that they did not need to go outside of Him for anything. 'To whom God would make known what is THE RICHES of the glory of THIS MYSTERY among the Gentiles WHICH IS CHRIST IN YOU, the hope of glory' (Colossians 1:27). The truth of this, known in power, is the sure and certain antidote for Laodicean pride, rationalistic theology, traditional religion, demon-possessed spiritualistic mediums, and every other form of opposition or counterfeit"—Alfred Mace.

In Christ all the treasures of wisdom and knowledge are hidden. **2:3** The Gnostics, of course, boasted of an understanding far surpassing anything that was found within the pages of divine revelation. Their wisdom was something in addition to that which was found in Christ or Christianity. But Paul is here saying that all the treasures of wisdom and knowledge are hidden in Christ, the Head. Therefore, there is no need for believers to go beyond what is written in the Scriptures. The treasures in Christ are hidden from unbelief; and even the believer needs to know Christ intimately to enter into them.

"Christ is *in* the believer as Head, center and resource. By the vastness of His unsearchable riches, by the pre-eminent wealth of His infinite greatness, by all that He is essentially as God, by all He has accomplished in creation and in redemption, by His personal, moral and official glories, He crowds out the whole army of professors, authors, mediums, critics, and all others arrayed against Him"—Selected. There is more in this verse than meets the eye. All knowledge is found in Christ. He is the incarnation of truth. He said, "I am the way, *the truth,* and the life." Nothing that is true will ever conflict with His words or His works. The difference between knowledge and wisdom has often been explained as follows: Knowledge is the understanding of truth, whereas wisdom is the ability to apply what truth has been learned.

PAUL'S WARNING (2:4)

Because all wisdom and knowledge are in Christ, Christians should not **2:4** be deluded with the persuasive speech of false cultists. If a man does not have the truth, then he must seek to attract a following through the clever presentation of his message. That is exactly what the heresies of our day seek to do. They argue from probabilities and build a system of teaching on deductions. On the other hand, if a man is preaching the truth of God, then he does not need to depend on such things as eloquence or clever arguments. The truth is its own best argument and, like a lion, will defend itself.

EXHORTATION TO STEDFASTNESS (2:5-7)

2:5 This verse shows how intimately aware the apostle Paul was of the problems and perils facing the Colossians. He pictures himself as a military officer looking over the assembled troops as they stand ready for inspection. The two words "order" and "stedfastness" are military terms. The first describes the orderly array of a company of soldiers, whereas the second pictures the solid flank which is presented by them. Paul rejoices as (in spirit though not in body) he beholds the manner in which the Colossians were standing true to the Word of God.

2:6 Now he encourages them to go on in the same manner in which they had originally begun. "As ye have therefore received Christ Jesus the Lord, so walk ye in Him." The emphasis here seems to be on the word "Lord." They had originally received Christ Jesus as Lord. In other words, they had acknowledged that in Him there was complete sufficiency. He was enough, not only for salvation, but for the whole of their Christian life. Now Paul urges the saints to go on acknowledging the Lordship of Christ. They should not stray from Him by accepting the teachings of men, however convincing they may sound. The word "walk" is one that is often used of the Christian life. It speaks of action and progress. You cannot walk and remain in the same place. So it is in the Christian life; we are either going forward or backward.

2:7 This verse is another one that is rather difficult to understand. The apostle seems to change his figures of speech almost more rapidly than we can follow. He first uses an expression from agriculture, then one from architecture. The expression "rooted" refers to what took place at the time of our conversion. It is as if the Lord Jesus Christ were the soil and we find our roots in Him, drawing all our nourishment from Him. This emphasizes, too, the importance of having our roots deep, so that when opposing winds should blow, we will not be moved (Matthew 13:5, 20, 21).

Then Paul switches to the figure of a building. "Built up in Him."

Here the Lord Jesus is suggested as the foundation, and we are being built on Him, the Rock of Ages (Luke 6:47-49). We were rooted once for all, but we are being built up.

"And stablished in the faith." It is difficult to determine what additional thought is given by this expression. We believe that the word "stablished" might also be translated "confirmed," and the thought is that this is a process that goes on continuously through the Christian life. The Colossians had been taught the fundamentals of Christianity by Epaphras. As they continued on in the Christian pathway, these precious truths would be continually confirmed in their hearts and lives. Conversely, 2 Peter 1:9 indicates that failure to progress in spiritual life results in doubt and loss of the joy and blessing of the gospel.

Paul concludes this description with the words "abounding therein with thanksgiving." He does not want the Christians to be coldly doctrinal, but he wants their hearts to be captivated by the marvelous truths of the gospel so that they in turn will overflow in praise and thankfulness to the Lord. Thanksgiving for the blessings of Christianity is a wonderful antidote against the poison of false doctrine.

Way translates this verse as follows: "Be like trees fast-rooted, like buildings steadily rising, feeling His presence about you, and even (for to this your education has led up) unshaken in your faith, and overflowing with thanksgiving."

When you have mastered this lesson, take the first part of Exam 4 (covering lesson 7), questions 1-10 on pages125-127(right after lesson 8)

Spiritual Perils

Colossians 2:8-23

IV. The peril of "philosophy" and deceitful teachings (v. 8).
V. The believer's resource in Christ (vv. 9-16).
   a. He is God in the fullest sense (v. 9).
   b. The believer is complete in Him (v. 10).
      (1) He has died with Christ—pictured by circumcision (v. 11).
      (2) He has been buried with Christ—pictured by baptism (v. 12).
      (3) He has risen with Christ—pictured by baptism (vv. 12, 13).
      (4) He has been forgiven all trespasses (v. 13).
      (5) He has been delivered from the ceremonies and ordinances of Judaism (v. 14).
      (6) His Christ has triumphed over evil spirits (v. 15).
VI. Warnings against:
   a. Legalism (vv. 16, 17).
   b. Mysticism (vv. 18, 19).
   c. Asceticism (vv. 20-23).

BEWARE OF "PHILOSOPHY" (2:8)

Now Paul is ready to deal directly with the specific errors that had **2:8** threatened the believers in the Lycus Valley, where Colosse was situated. The King James Version says, "Beware lest any man spoil you through philosophy and vain deceit." The word "spoil" means to rob. False teachings seek to rob men of what is worthwhile, but offer nothing substantial in its place. "Philosophy" means literally "the love of wisdom." It is not evil in itself, but becomes evil when men seek wisdom apart from the Lord Jesus Christ. Here the word is used to describe man's attempt to find out by his own intellect and research those things which can only be known by divine revelation (1 Corinthians 2:14). It is evil because it exalts human reason above God and worships the creature more than the Creator. It is characteristic of the modernists or liberals of our day, with their boasted intellectualism and rationalism. "Vain deceit" refers to the false and valueless teachings of those who profess to offer secret truths to an inner circle of people. There is really nothing to it. But it gathers a following by catering to man's curiosity. Also it appeals to their vanity by making them members of the "select few."

The philosophy and vain deceit which Paul attacks are "after the tradition of men, after the rudiments of the world, and not after Christ." The tradition of men here means religious teachings which have been invented by men but which have no foundation in the Scriptures. (A tradition is a fixation of a custom which began as a convenience, or which suited some particular circumstance.) The rudiments of the world refer to Jewish rituals, ceremonies, and ordinances by which men hoped to obtain God's favor. "The Law of Moses had served its purpose as a type of things to come. It had been a 'primary school' to prepare the heart for the coming Christ. To return to it now would be to play into the hands of the false teachers who conspired to use a discarded system to displace the Son of God"—Daily Notes of the Scripture Union. Paul would have the Colossians test all teaching by whether or not it agreed with the doctrines of the Lord Jesus Christ. Phillips' translation of this verse is helpful: "Be careful that nobody spoils your faith through intellectualism or high sounding nonsense. Such stuff is at best founded on men's ideas of the nature of the world, and disregards Christ!"

THE GODHEAD OF JESUS (2:9)

It is marvelous to see how the apostle Paul constantly brings his readers back to the Person of Christ. Here he gives one of the most sublime and unmistakable verses in the Bible on the deity of the Lord Jesus Christ. "For in Him dwelleth all the fulness of the Godhead bodily." Note the intended accumulation of evidence as to the fact that Christ is God. First of all, you have His deity: "For in Him dwelleth . . . *the Godhead bodily.*" Secondly, you have what someone has called the amplitude of deity: "For in Him dwelleth *the fulness of the Godhead bodily.*" Finally, you have what has been called the absolute completeness of deity: "For in Him dwelleth *all the fulness of the Godhead bodily.*" (This is an effective answer to the various forms of gnosticism that deny the deity of the Lord Jesus—Christian Science, Jehovah's Witnesses, Unity, Theosophy, Christadelphianism, etc.)

Vincent says, "The verse contains two distinct assertions: (1) That the fulness of the Godhead eternally dwells in Christ . . .; (2) The fulness of the Godhead dwells in Him as one having a human body. . . ." Many of the cults mentioned above would admit that some form of divinity dwelt in Jesus. This verse is identifying "all the fulness of the Godhead" with Him, in His manhood. The argument is clear—if there is such a sufficiency in the Person of the Lord Jesus Christ, why be satisfied with teachings which slight or ignore Him?

WE ARE COMPLETE IN HIM (2:10-15)

The apostle is still trying to impress upon his readers the all-sufficiency of the Lord Jesus Christ, and of the perfect standing which they have in Him. It is a marvelous expression of the grace of God that the truth of verse 10 should follow that of verse 9. In Christ dwells all the fulness of the Godhead bodily, and the believer is complete in Him. This does not mean, of course, that the believer is indwelt by all the fulness of the Godhead. The only One of Whom that was ever true, or shall ever be true, is the Lord Jesus Christ. But what this verse teaches is that the believer has in Christ all that is needed for life and godliness. Spurgeon gives a good definition of our completeness. He says we are (1) Complete without the aid of Jewish Ceremony. (2) Complete without the help of philosophy. (3) Complete without the inventions of superstition. (4) Complete without human merit.

This One in Whom we are complete is the Head of all principality and power. As we know, the Gnostics were greatly taken up with the subject of angels. Mention of this is made later on in this chapter. But Christ is head over all the angelic beings, and it would be ridiculous to be occupied with angels when we can have the Creator of angels as the object of our affections and enjoy communion with Him.

2:11   Circumcision was the typical rite of Judaism. It was a minor surgical operation in which the knife was applied to the flesh of the male child. Spiritually it signified death to the flesh, or a putting aside of the evil, corrupt, unregenerate nature of man. Unfortunately, the Jewish people became occupied with the literal ceremony but neglected its spiritual meaning. In trying to achieve favor with God through ceremonies and good works, they were saying, in effect, that there was something in human flesh which could please God. Nothing could be farther from the truth.

In the verse before us physical circumcision is not in view, but rather that spiritual circumcision which is true of everyone who has put his faith and trust in the Lord Jesus. This is clear from the expression "the circumcision made without hands." What the verse is teaching is this: Every believer is circumcised by the circumcision of Christ. The circumcision of Christ refers to His death on the Cross of Calvary. The thought is that when the Lord Jesus died, the believer died also. He died to sin (Romans 6:11), to the law, to self (Galatians 2:19, 20), and to the world (Galatians 6:14). (This circumcision was "made without hands" in the sense that human hands can have no part in it by way of merit. Man cannot deserve or earn it. It is God's work.) Thus he has put off the body of the flesh. (The expression "the body of the sins of the flesh" is more accurately translated in the A.S.V. "the body of the flesh.") In other words, when a person is saved, he becomes associated with Christ in His death, and renounces any hope of earning or deserving salvation through fleshly efforts. "Our Lord's death has not only put away the fruit, but condemned and set aside the very root

114

which bore it"—Samuel Ridout.

Paul now turns from the subject of circumcision to that of baptism. Just as circumcision speaks of death to the flesh, even so baptism speaks of the burial of the old man. Thus we read, "Buried with Him in baptism, wherein also ye are risen with Him through the faith of the operation of God, Who hath raised Him from the dead." The teaching here is that we have not only died with Christ, but we have been buried with Him. This was typified at our baptism. It took place at the time of our conversion, but we expressed it in public confession when we went into the waters of baptism. Baptism is burial, the burial of all that we were as children of Adam. In baptism we acknowledge that nothing in ourselves could ever please God, and so we are putting the flesh out of God's sight forever. But it does not end with burial. Not only have we been crucified with Christ and buried with Him, but we have also risen with Him to walk in newness of life. All of this takes place at the time of our conversion. It is through faith in the working of God, Who raised Christ from the dead. 2:12

The apostle Paul now makes the application of all this to the Colossians. Before their conversion, they had been dead in their sins. This means that because of their sins, they were spiritually dead toward God. It does not mean that their spirits were dead, but simply that there was no motion in their spirits toward God and there was nothing they could do to win God's favor. Not only were they dead in sins, but also Paul speaks of the uncircumcision of their flesh. Uncircumcision is often used in the New Testament to describe the Gentile peoples. The Colossians had been Gentiles. They had not been members of God's earthly people, the Jews. Therefore, they had been in a position of distance from God, and had given full reign to the flesh with its lusts. But when they heard the gospel and believed on the Lord Jesus Christ, they had been quickened together with Christ, and all their trespasses had been forgiven. In other words, what had really happened to the Colossians was that their whole manner of life had been changed. Their history as sinners had come to an end, and now they were new creatures in Christ Jesus. They were living on the resurrection side. Therefore they should say "goodbye" to all that characterized them as men in the flesh. 2:13

2:14   The apostle Paul now goes on to describe something else that was included in the work of Christ. "Blotting out the handwriting of ordinances that was against us, which was contrary to us, and took it out of the way, nailing it to His cross." "The handwriting of ordinances that was against us" describes the law. In a sense, the Ten Commandments were against us, condemning us because we did not keep them perfectly. But the apostle Paul is thinking not only about the Ten Commandments, but also about the ceremonial law that was given to Israel. In the ceremonial law, there were all kinds of commandments with regard to holy days, foods, and other religious rituals. These were all a part of the prescribed religion of the Jews. They pointed forward to the coming of the Lord Jesus. They were shadows of His Person and of His Work. In His death on the Cross, He took all this out of the way, nailing it to His cross and canceling it as a bill is canceled when the debt is paid. "By the death of Christ on the Cross, the law which condemned men lost its penal authority, inasmuch as Christ by His death endured for man the curse of the law and became the end of the law"—Meyer. "The law is not dead, but we have died to it"—Wm. Kelly.

2:15   By His death on the Cross and His subsequent resurrection and ascension, the Lord Jesus also conquered evil powers, making a show of them openly, and triumphing over them. We believe that this is the same triumph that is described in Ephesians 4, where the Lord Jesus is said to have led captivity captive. His death, burial, resurrection, and ascension were a glorious triumph over all the hosts of hell and of Satan. As He passed up through the atmosphere on His way back to heaven, He passed through the very domain of the one who is the prince of the power of the air.

Perhaps this verse carries special comfort for those who have been converted from demonism but who might still be obsessed with a fear of evil spirits. There is nothing to fear if we are in Christ, because He has triumphed over principalities and powers.

BEWARE OF LEGALISM (2:16, 17)

2:16   Once again the apostle Paul is ready to make the application of what he has just been stating. We might summarize the foregoing as follows: The Colossians had died to all efforts to please God by the flesh. They had not only died, but they had been buried with Christ and had risen with Christ to a new kind of life. Therefore they should be done forever with the Judaizers and Gnostics, who were trying to draw them back to the very things to which the Colossians had died. "Let no man therefore judge you in meat, or in drink, or in respect of an holyday, or of the new moon, or of the sabbath days." All human religions place men under bondage to ordinances, rules, regulations, and a religious calendar. This calendar usually includes annual observances (holy days), monthly festivals (new moons), or weekly holidays (sabbaths). The expression "let no man therefore judge you" means that a Christian cannot be justly condemned by others if, for instance, he eats pork, or if he fails to observe religious festivals or holy days. Some false cults, such as spiritism, insist on their members abstaining from meats. For centuries Friday was supposed to be a meatless day for multitudes. Many churches require abstinence from certain foods during Lent. Others, like the Mormons, say that a person cannot be a member in good standing if he drinks tea or coffee. Still others, notably the Seventh Day Adventists, insist that a person must keep the Sabbath in order to please God. The Christian is not under such ordinances.

In connection with the Sabbath, the student should be clear on the following points:

1. The Sabbath is the seventh day of the week. God rested from the work of creation on that day (Genesis 2:2), and later ordered the children of Israel to set it apart as a day of rest (Exodus 20:8-11). The penalty for failing to keep it holy was death (Numbers 15: 32-36).

2. Neither the keeping of the Sabbath nor any of the rest of the Ten Commandments were ever intended by God as a way of salvation (Acts 13:39; Romans 3:20; Galatians 2:16, 21; 3:11). Their purpose was to reveal to man his utter sinfulness, and to cast him on the grace, mercy, and love of God (Romans 3:20; 5:20; 7:7; Galatians 3:19).

3. In His death on the Cross, Christ paid the penalty of the broken law. Therefore, those who trust in Him are no longer under the law, but under grace (Romans 6:14; 2 Corinthians 3:7-11). This does not mean that they are free to sin. A Christian does not want to sin. But his motive for holy living is no longer fear of punishment, as under the law, but love to Christ, Who died for him.

4. A Christian is not required to keep the Sabbath. Nine of the Ten Commandments are repeated in the New Testament as instruction in righteousness for the people of God. The only one that is not repeated is the one concerning the Sabbath. Nowhere in the New Testament are Christians taught to observe the Sabbath.

5. The Christian does not "keep" any day with the idea of obtaining holiness or pleasing God. To the believer, all days are holy.

6. However, he sees that the Lord's Day, or the first day of the week, is spoken of in the New Testament as the day (a) when our Lord rose from the dead (John 20:1); (b) when the Holy Spirit was given (Leviticus 23:15, 16; Acts 2:1); (c) when the disciples gathered together to break bread (Acts 20:7); and (d) when the early Christians were instructed to set aside their offerings to the Lord (1 Corinthians 16:1, 2).

7. The Sabbath was not changed to the Lord's Day. The two are entirely distinct. The Sabbath was the seventh day; the Lord's Day is the first. The Sabbath closed the week, looking forward to a rest still future. The Lord's Day opens the week with a rest that has already been obtained for believers.

   The Sabbath was a day of duty. The Lord's Day is a day of privilege. Most of us do not have to work in our usual employment on the Lord's Day, and can give it to the Lord for worship and service in a way that is not possible during the remainder of the week. In thinking of the Lord's Day, the question is not "Would it be wrong for me to do such and such?" but "How can I use this day to the best advantage for Christ?" "The true character of the

Lord's Day is illustrated in our Lord's use of it. He comforted weeping Mary; walked seven miles with two perplexed disciples, giving a Bible reading by the way; sent messages to other disciples; had a private interview with backslidden Peter; and imparted the Holy Spirit to the men in the upper chamber"—Scofield. One final consideration! Christians should be careful not to do anything on the Lord's Day that might prove an offense or a cause of stumbling to others.

The Jewish religious observances were a shadow of things to come. **2:17** But the body is Christ's. They were instituted in the Old Testament as a pre-picture. For instance, the Sabbath was given as a type of the rest which would be the portion of all who believed on the Lord Jesus Christ. Now that the Lord Jesus has come, why should men continue to be occupied with the shadows? It is the same as being occupied with a picture when the person is present.

BEWARE OF MYSTICISM (2:18-19)

It is rather difficult to know the exact meaning of this verse, because **2:18** we are not fully acquainted with all that the Gnostics taught. Perhaps it means that these people pretended to be so humble that they would not dare to approach God directly. Perhaps the Gnostics taught that they must approach God through angels, and so in their supposed humility they worshipped angels rather than the Lord. We have something similar to this in the world today. There are those who say that they would not think of praying directly to God or to the Lord Jesus, and so they pray to the mother of Jesus or some other departed person who has been designated a "saint." This seems to be a voluntary humility on their part and a worshipping of a created being. Christians should not allow anyone to rob them of their reward by such unscriptural practices. The Word is clear that there is "one mediator between God and men, the man Christ Jesus" (1 Timothy 2:5).

The apostle Paul goes on with another expression that is difficult to understand: "intruding into those things which he hath not seen."

In most versions the "not" is omitted. For instance, the American Standard Version says: "Dwelling in the things which he hath seen." The Gnostics professed to have deep secret mysteries, and in order to learn what these mysteries were, a person had to be initiated. Perhaps the secrets included many so-called visions. Those who were members of the inner circle were naturally proud of their secret knowledge. Paul therefore adds, "Vainly puffed up by his fleshly mind." They took a superior attitude toward others and created the impression that one could be happy only through entering into these deep secrets. We might pause here to say that much of this is characteristic of the secret fraternal organizations of our day. The Christian who is walking in fellowship with his Lord will have neither time nor sympathy for such organizations.

The important point to notice in this verse is that the various religious practices of these men were performed according to their own will. They had no scriptural authority. They did not act in subjection to Christ. They became vainly puffed up by the mind of their flesh because they were doing exactly what they themselves wanted to do, in independence of the Lord; yet their conduct appeared to be humble and religious.

2:19   "And not holding the Head." The Lord Jesus is here spoken of as the Head of the body. "To hold the Head" means to live with the consciousness that Christ is Head, drawing the supply of all our needs from His exhaustless resources, and doing all for His glory. It means looking to the Lord in glory for sustenance and direction, and keeping in touch with Him. This is further explained in the expression that follows: "From which all the body by joints and bands having nourishment ministered, and knit together, increaseth with the increase of God." The various parts of the human body are connected together by joints and ligaments. The body in turn is joined to the head. The body looks to the head for guidance and direction. That is just the thought that the apostle Paul is emphasizing here. The members of Christ's body on earth should find all their satisfaction and sufficiency in Him, and not be lured away by the convincing arguments of these false teachers.

"Holding the Head" emphasizes the necessity for a moment-by-moment dependence on the Lord. Yesterday's help will not do for today. "We cannot grind the grain with the water that has passed over the dam." It should also be added here that where Christians do hold the Head, the result will be spontaneous action which will coordinate with other members of the body.

BEWARE OF ASCETICISM (2:20-23)

The rudiments of the world, as used in this verse, refer to rituals and **2:20** ordinances. For instance, the rituals of the Old Testament were rudiments of the world in the sense that they taught the elementary principles of religion, the ABC's (Galatians 4:9-11). Perhaps Paul is also thinking of the rituals and ordinances connected with Gnosticism and other religions. In particular, the apostle is dealing with asceticism, springing from a Judaism which had already lost its standing with God, or from Gnosticism or any other cult which never had any standing with God. Since the Colossians had died with Christ, Paul asks them why there was still a desire to subject themselves to such ordinances; to do so would be to forget that they had severed their ties with the world. Perhaps the question will arise in some minds, "If a Christian is dead to ordinances, why does he still retain baptism and the Lord's Supper?" The most obvious answer is that these two ordinances of the Christian Church are taught in the New Testament. However, they are not "means of grace," making us more fit for heaven or helping us to gain merit before God. Rather they are simple acts of obedience to the Lord, indicating respectively, identification with Christ, and remembrance of Him in His death. They are not so much laws to be kept as privileges to be enjoyed.

This verse is better understood if we supply the words "such as" **2:21** at the beginning. In other words, Paul is saying in verse 20, "Why then, as though living in the world, do ye subject yourselves to ordinances (21), such as, touch not; taste not; handle not." Strangely enough, some have taught that Paul was here *commanding* the Colossians to "touch not; taste not; handle not." This, of course, is the very opposite of the meaning of the passage.

It should be mentioned here that many authorities believe that the order of the clauses in this verse should be—"Handle not; Neither taste; Nor even touch" (William Kelly). This order seems to describe an increasing severity in the practice of asceticism.

2:22 The meaning is still further explained in verse 22. These are prohibitions which are man-made, as is indicated by the expression "after the commandments and doctrines of men." Is this the essence of true religion, to be occupied with meats and drinks, rather than with the living Christ Himself?

Weymouth translates verses 20-22 as follows: "If you have died with Christ and have escaped from the world's rudimentary notions, why, as though your life still belonged to the world, do you submit to such precepts as 'Do not handle this'; 'Do not taste that'; 'Do not touch that other thing'—referring to things which are all intended to be used up and to perish—in obedience to mere human injunctions and teachings?"

2:23 These practices of man's religion all create a seeming appearance of wisdom in will worship, and humility, and severity to the body. "Will worship" means that these people adopt a form of worship according to their own ideas of what is right, rather than according to God's Word. They seem to be religious but it is not true Christianity. Humility has already been explained: they pretend to be too humble to approach God directly, and so they use angelic mediators. "Neglecting of the body" refers to the practice of asceticism. It is the belief that through self-denial or through self-torture, man can achieve a higher state of holiness. This is found in Yoga (Hinduism) and other mystical religions of the East.

What is the value of all these practices? Perhaps it is best expressed in the A.S.V. translation of the closing part of this verse: "But are not of any value against the indulgence of the flesh." All of these put on a fine appearance outwardly, but they do not succeed in checking the indulgence of the flesh. (Even the well-intentioned temperance pledges fail to achieve their goal.) Every false system utterly fails to make men better. While creating the impression that there is something the flesh can do to merit God's favor, they are unable to restrain the passions and lusts of the flesh. The Christian attitude is that we have died to the flesh with all its passions and lusts, and we henceforth live to the glory of God. We do this, not out of fear of punishment, but rather out of love to the One Who gave Himself for us. "It is love that makes us really free to do right. Love makes the choice easy. Love makes the face of duty beautiful. Love makes it sweet to keep up with Christ. Love makes the service of goodness freedom"—A. T. Robertson.

Phillips' translation of the latter part of verse 23 gives a slightly different meaning: "But in actual practice they do honour, not to God, but to man's own pride."[1]

---

[1] *New Testament in Modern English.* New York: Macmillan Company, 1959. Used by permission of the publisher.

When you are ready, complete Exam 4 by answering questions 11-20 on pages 128-130. (You should have already answered questions 1-10 as part of your study of lesson 7.)

PHILIPPIANS, COLOSSIANS and PHILEMON

Exam 4
Lessons 7, 8

Name _____
            (print plainly)

Exam
Grade_____

Address _____

City _____ State _____ Zip Code _____ Class Number _____

Instructor _____

LESSON 7

In the blank space in the right-hand margin write the letter of the correct answer. (50 points)

1. The "afflictions of Christ" which Paul rejoiced to help "fill up" in his own sufferings should be regarded as
    a. the atoning sufferings of Christ
    b. the sufferings Christians experience and in which Christ still shares
    c. the sufferings of unsaved people for whom Christ died
    d. the sufferings of the unsaved   _____

2. Paul's ministry consisted of
    a. preaching Christ to the lost
    b. teaching believers vital spiritual truths
    c. both preaching to the lost and teaching believers
    d. pastoring various local churches as called by their congregations to be their minister   _____

3. When Paul speaks of "the dispensation of God" committed to him he is referring to
    a. the age of grace as distinguished from the age of law
    b. the division of God's administration of the earth into a series of major dispensations or periods and the truth of which he was first to recognize and preach
    c. the truths which were revealed exclusively to him
    d. his stewardship of those truths entrusted to him especially in relation to the Gentiles   _____

4. How did Paul "fulfil" or "complete" the Word of God? By
   a. declaring the whole counsel of God
   b. announcing the great mysteries of the faith which complete the subjects covered by the New Testament
   c. doing both the above
   d. adding the last book to the New Testament (even though that book is not last in the present order of New Testament books)

5. Which of the following is *NOT* a part of "the mystery"?
   a. The Church, the body of Christ, is composed of all true believers since Pentecost
   b. The Church is related to the Lord Jesus as a body is related to its head
   c. There is no distinction in the Church between Jew and Gentile
   d. Gentiles can be saved as well as Jews

6. The particular aspect of the mystery that Paul was emphasizing to the Colossians was that
   a. Christ is the end of the law for righteousness to everyone that believes
   b. Christ dwells in the heart of the believer even though he be a Gentile
   c. Christ will not only raise the dead at the second advent, but living believers will be caught up alive to meet Him in the air
   d. Christ is seated at God's right hand to intercede for His own

7. Paul's goals, as an evangelist, pastor and teacher, included
   a. warning every man
   b. teaching every man
   c. presenting every man perfect in Christ
   d. all the above

8. The "conflict" of which Paul speaks in this epistle was
   a. a running battle he had with unbelieving Jews in city after city
   b. his constant struggle against the inroads of error
   c. a continual spiritual warfare in prayer
   d. his unceasing struggle with legalistic brethren

9. Which of the following verses best refuted the claims of the Gnostics that they possessed an understanding far superior to anything found in the Bible?
   a. Colossians 1:23
   b. Colossians 1:25
   c. Colossians 2:3
   d. Colossians 2:5   _____

10. Paul exhorted the Colossians to be steadfast and in so doing employed the language of
   'a. a mother correcting her children
   b. a nurse admonishing a patient
   c. a military officer inspecting his troops
   d. a shepherd assembling his flock   _____

WHAT DO YOU SAY?

Have you ever encountered the "enticing words" of a cult propagandist? Describe your contact and your reaction.

_____

_____

_____

_____

_____

_____

_____

_____

_____

_____

_____

LESSON 8

In the blank space in the right-hand margin write the letter of the correct answer. (50 points)

11. When Paul warned against philosophy he was
   a. revealing an ingrained prejudice against learning and scholarship
   b. warning against placing human reasoning above divine revelation
   c. referring to the valueless teachings of those who professed to offer secret truths to a select inner circle
   d. saying that "ignorant and unlearned men" should always be given priority in the Church   _____

12. Paul warned the Colossians against Jewish rituals, ceremonies and ordinances in the expression
   a. "the rudiments of the world"
   b. "the traditions of men"
   c. "the rent veil"
   d. "the beggarly elements"   _____

13. According to the Jehovah's Witnesses the Word (logos) is "a god" and was made human as the man Jesus. He was "not an incarnation in flesh but was flesh . . . no longer a spirit although having a spiritual or a heavenly past and background." Which of the following passages refutes such teaching? (You may look up the references in your Bible.)
   a. John 1:1-3, 14
   b. Colossians 1:15-17; 2:9
   c. Hebrews 1:1-3, 7-8
   d. all the above   _____

14. According to Colossians 2:11, circumcision
   a. should be administered to Christians as part of the cultural heritage Christianity has received from Judaism
   b. signifies the way in which God deals with "the old man"
   c. is fulfilled for the believer in Christ's death on the cross where the flesh was dealt with fully and to God's satisfaction
   d. ought to be practiced by Christian Jews but need not be practiced by Gentile Christians   _____

128

15. Which of the following best states the case so far as the Christian is concerned? The law of God

a. is dead and has no relationship to the Christian believer

b. is not dead but the believer has been discharged from its penal authority

c. was nailed to the cross

d. was binding on all mankind and still is God's basis for dealing with men _____

16. Which of the following truly belongs to the New Testament concept of the Christian faith? The

a. observance of one day in seven as a Sabbath rest

b. abstinence from certain types of food

c. keeping of certain days in the Christian calendar as holy

d. complete freedom of the believer from ritual worship _____

17. Of all the commandments contained in the Decalog (the Ten Commandments) the one *NOT* repeated in the New Testament as an instruction in righteousness for the people of God is the commandment to

a. avoid worshipping graven images

b. keep the Sabbath day

c. honor one's parents

d. abstain from covetousness _____

18. Worshipping angels is

a. a right and proper practice for those who are so conscious of their failings that they dare not approach God directly

b. an unscriptural practice

c. a practice once common in the church but now entirely absent from all churches in Christendom

d. a Judaistic concept and therefore of some, even if little, value _____

19. Baptism and the Lord's Supper are

a. part of our Judaistic heritage as Christians

b. customs which cannot be reconciled with Colossians 2:20

c. Gnostic in character and therefore suspect

d. simple acts of obedience and excluded from Paul's censure of "the rudiments"

e. "means of grace" and intended to help us accumulate merit before God _____

20. Paul

    a. recommends long fasts as an excellent way of checking fleshly indulgences

    b. taught that the body ought to be neglected since it is the soul and the spirit which are important

    c. gave the Colossians a list of "do's and don'ts" to enable them better to regulate their lives

    d. saw clearly that purely human prohibitions actually minister to human pride and do not honor God   _____

WHAT DO YOU SAY?

Describe one teaching or practice of a cult which you can now see to be in error as a result of this study.

_____

_____

_____

_____

_____

Lesson Nine

New Lives For Old

Colossians 3:1-17

I. The believer's new life (vv. 1-4).
   a. New position—risen with Christ (v. 1).
   b. New responsibilities (vv. 1, 2).
      (1) To seek the things above (v. 1).
      (2) To set affections on heavenly things (v. 2).
   c. New address—hid with Christ in God (v. 3).
   d. New hope—manifested with Him in glory (v. 4).

II. Putting off the old man (vv. 5-9).
   a. Unholy love (vv. 5-7).
   b. Wicked hate (v. 8).
   c. Dishonest speech (v. 9).

III. Putting on the new man (vv. 10-17).
   a. Tender mercies (v. 12).
   b. Kindness (v. 12).
   c. Lowliness (v. 12).
   d. Meekness (v. 12).
   e. Longsuffering (v. 12).
   f. Forbearing (v. 13).
   g. Forgiving (v. 13).
   h. Loving (v. 14).
   i. Monitored by the peace of Christ (v. 15).
   j. Filled with the word of Christ (v. 16).
   k. Doing all in the Name of the Lord Jesus (v. 17).

3:1   "If then ye were raised together with Christ, seek the things that are above, where Christ is, seated on the right hand of God" (A.S.V.). The "if" of this verse does not express any doubt in the mind of the apostle Paul. It is what has been called the "if" of argument, and might just as well have been translated "since." Since then ye were raised together with Christ. . . .

As mentioned in the previous chapter, the believer is seen as having died with Christ, having been buried with Him, and having risen with Him from among the dead. The spiritual meaning of all this is that we have said good-by to the former way of life, and have entered upon a completely new type of life, that is, the life of the risen Lord Jesus Christ. Because we have been raised together with Christ, we should seek those things which are above. We are still on earth, but we should be cultivating heavenly ways.

3:2   The Christian should not be earth-bound in his outlook. He should view things not as they appear to the natural eye but in reference to their importance to God and for eternity. The word "affection" is more correctly "mind," with the thought of directing the mind. Vincent suggests that "seek" marks the practical striving, in verse 1, and that "set your mind" in verse 2 describes the inward impulse and disposition. The expression "set your mind" is similar to that in Philippians 3:19— "who *mind* earthly things." "The baptized life means that the Christian is seeking heaven and thinking heaven. His feet are upon the earth, but his head is with the stars. He is living like a citizen of heaven here on earth"—A. T. Robertson.

During the last war, a young Christian enthusiastically reported to an older servant of Christ, "I understand our bombers were over the enemy's cities again last night." To this, the older believer replied, "I did not know that the church of God had bombers." He obviously was looking at things from the divine standpoint, rather than taking pleasure in the ruthless slaughter of innocent women and children.

"The counterpart to our identification with Christ in His death is our identification with Him in His resurrection. The effect of the first is to disconnect us from man's world, man's religion, man's wisdom.

The effect of the other is to put us into touch with God's world and with all that is there. The first four verses of chapter 3 unfold the blessedness into which we are introduced"—F. B. Hole.

When the apostle Paul says that the believer has died, he is referring to position, and not to practice. Because of our identification with Christ in His death, God wants us to consider ourselves as having died with Him. Our own hearts are always ready to dispute this fact, because we feel so very much alive to sin and temptation. But the wonderful thing is that as we by faith reckon ourselves to have died with Christ, it becomes a moral reality in our lives. If we live as those who have died, then our lives will become increasingly conformed to the life of the Lord Jesus Christ. Of course, we will never reach perfection in this life, but it is a process that should be going on in every believer.

Not only have we died, but also our life is hid with Christ in God. The things that concern and interest the worldly man are found on this planet on which we live. However, the things that are of greatest concern to the believer are all bound up in the Person of the Lord Jesus Christ. His destiny and ours are inseparable. Paul's thought is that since our life is hid with Christ in God, we should not be occupying ourselves with the petty things of this world, and especially of the religious world about us.

But there is another thought connected with the expression "your life is hid with Christ in God." The world does not see our spiritual life. Men do not understand us. They think it is strange that we do not live like they do. They do not comprehend our thoughts, our motives, or our ways. Just as it is said of the Holy Spirit that the world "seeth him not, neither knoweth him," so it is with our spiritual life; it is hid with Christ in God. 1 John 3:1 tells us, "Therefore the world knoweth us not, because it knew Him not." The real separation from the world lies in the fact that the world does not understand, but rather misunderstands the believer.

To climax his description of the believer's portion in Christ, the apostle now looks on to Christ's coming again. When He Who is our Life shall be manifested, then we shall also be manifested with Him in glory. At the present time we are raised with Him and enjoying a life that is not seen or understood by men. But the day is coming when the Lord Jesus will return for His saints. Then we shall be manifested with Him in glory. Men will understand us then and realize why we behaved as we did.

OFF WITH THE OLD MAN (3:5-9)

3:5 In verse 3, we were told that we died. Here we are told to mortify therefore our members which are on the earth. In these two verses we have a very clear illustration of the difference between a believer's standing and state. His standing is that he has died. His state should be that of reckoning himself dead to sin by mortifying his members which are upon the earth. Our standing is what we are in Christ. Our state is what we are in ourselves. Our standing is the free gift of God through faith in the Lord Jesus Christ. Our state represents our response to God's grace.

The student should notice here also the difference between law and grace. God does not say, "If you live a life of freedom from sin, then I will give you a position of death with Christ." That would be law. Our position would depend on our own efforts, and needless to say, no one would ever attain that position. Instead of that, God says, "I freely give to all who believe on the Lord Jesus a position of favor in my sight. Now go out and live a life that is consistent with such a high calling." That is grace!

When the apostle says that we should put to death our members which are upon the earth, he does not mean that we should literally destroy any of the members of our physical body. The expression is a figurative one, and is explained in the phrases that follow. The word "members" is used to signify the various forms of lust and hatred that are enumerated.

"Fornication" is generally used to describe unlawful sexual intercourse or immorality. Sometimes it is synonymous with adultery (Matthew 5:32; 19:9), where the sin is committed by a married person. At other times it means this same sin committed by an unmarried person (Matthew 15:19; Mark 7:21). "Uncleanness" refers to impurity of thought, word, or action. It speaks of moral filth rather than physical dirtiness here. "Inordinate affection" denotes strong and unbridled passion. "Evil concupiscence" speaks of intense and oftentimes violent lust. "Covetousness" in general means greediness or the desire to have more, but here it may refer especially to unholy desire for the satisfaction of sexual appetite.

It is often pointed out that this list begins with acts and moves on to motives. The various forms of sexual sin are described, then they are traced to their lair, namely, the covetous heart of man. The Word of God is clear in teaching that there is nothing inherently wrong in sex. God made man with the power for reproduction. But the sin comes when those things which God has so graciously bestowed upon His creatures are used for vile, illicit purposes. Sexual sin was the cardinal offense of the pagan world in Paul's day, and doubtless it still holds first place. Where believers are not yielded to the Holy Spirit, sexual sins often come into their lives and prove their downfall.

Men think that they can commit these outrageous sins and escape **3:6** punishment. The heavens seem to be silent, and man increases in his boldness. But God is not mocked. The wrath of God comes down upon the sons of disobedience for these things. (Actually the words "upon the sons of disobedience" are not found in many manuscripts, but they do occur in the companion passage, Ephesians 5:6.) These sins have their consequences in this present life; men reap in their own bodies the results of sexual immorality. In addition they will reap a terrible harvest of judgment in a day yet future.

Paul reminds the Colossians that they once indulged in these sins **3:7** in the days before their conversion. But the grace of God had come in and delivered them from impurity. That was a chapter in their life which was now covered by the blood of Christ. They now had a new life which empowered them to live for God. See Galatians 5:25—"If we live in the Spirit, let us also walk in the Spirit."

Since they had been redeemed at such tremendous cost, they **3:8** should now put all these things away. Not only does the apostle refer to the various forms of unholy lust listed in verse five, but also to the types of wicked hatred which he is about to enumerate.

"Anger" is, of course, a strong spirit of dislike or animosity, a vengeful spirit, a settled feeling of hatred. "Wrath" describes an intense form of anger, probably involving violent outbursts. "Malice" is wicked conduct toward another with the idea of harming his person or his reputation. It is an unreasonable dislike that takes pleasure in seeing others suffer. "Blasphemy" here means railing, that is, strong, intemperate language used against another. It means scolding in a harsh, insolent manner. "Filthy communication" means shameful speaking, and describes that which is lewd, indecent, or corrupt. It is disgraceful, impure language.

In this catalog of sin the apostle goes from motives to acts. Bitterness starts in the human heart and then manifests itself in the various ways which have been described.

3:9   Here again in verse 9 the apostle is saying in effect, "Let your state be consistent with your standing." You have put off the old man; now put him off practically by refraining from lies. Lying is one of the things that belongs to the old man, and it has no place in the life of the child of God. Every day in our lives we are tempted to distort the truth. It may be by withholding information on an income tax form, or by cheating on an examination, or even by exaggerating the details of a story. Lying becomes doubly serious when we injure another by a false statement, or by creating a false impression.

ON WITH THE NEW MAN (3:10-17)

3:10   Not only have we put off the old man, but we have put on the new man, which is renewed in knowledge after the image of Him who created him. Just as the old man refers to all that we were as sons of Adam, with an unregenerate nature, so the new man refers to our new position as children of God. There has been a new creation, and we are new creatures. God's purpose is that this new man should ever be growing more and more like the Lord Jesus Christ. We should never be satisfied with our present attainments, but should always press on to the goal of increasing conformity to the Savior. He is our example and the rule of our lives. In a coming day, when we stand before the judgment seat of Christ, we will be judged not by how much better our lives were than others but rather by how our life measured up to the life of the Lord Jesus Himself.

"The image of God is not seen in the shape of our bodies, but in the beauty of the renewed mind and heart. Holiness, love, humility, meekness, kindness, and forgivingness—these make up the divine character"—Selected from Daily Notes of the Scripture Union.

In the new creation of which the apostle has been speaking, "there is neither Greek nor Jew, circumcision nor uncircumcision, Barbarian, Scythian, bond nor free: but Christ is all, and in all." This means that differences of nationality, religion, culture, and social level are not the things that count. As far as standing before God is concerned, all believers are on the same level, and in local church fellowship this same attitude should be adopted. 3:11

This does not mean that there are no distinctions in the church. Some have the gift of evangelist, some of pastor, and some of teacher. Some men are elders in the church and some are deacons. Thus, the verse does not disparage proper distinctions.

Neither should the verse be taken to teach that the distinctions listed have been abolished in the world. Such, of course, is not the case. There is still the Greek and the Jew, Greek here standing for the Gentile peoples in general. There is the circumcision and the uncircumcision. These two expressions are generally used in the New Testament to describe Jew and Gentile respectively. However, here they might refer more particularly to the ritual itself as practiced by the Jewish people, and as disregarded by the Gentiles.

There is still the Barbarian and the Scythian. These two expressions are not here set in contrast to one another. The Scythians were barbarians, but were generally considered to be the more extreme form; they were the wildest and most savage of the barbarians. The final contrast is between bond and free. Bond here, of course, refers to those held in bonds, or slaves, whereas free refers to those who never had been in bondage, but were born free. For the Christian these worldly distinctions are no longer of importance. It is Christ who really counts. He is everything to the believer and in everything. He represents the center and circumference of the Christian's life.

"The three words—Christ is all—are the essence and substance of

Christianity. If our hearts can really go along with them, it is well with our souls. . . . Many give Christ a certain place in their religion but not the place which God intended Him to fill. Christ alone is not 'all in all' to their souls. No! It is either Christ and the church—or Christ and the sacraments—or Christ and His ordained ministers—or Christ and their own repentance—or Christ and their own goodness—or Christ and their own prayers—or Christ and their own sincerity and charity, on which they practically rest their souls"—Ryle.

3:12   In verse 10, the apostle said that we have put on the new man. Now he gives some practical ways in which this can be done in our everyday lives. First of all, he addresses the Colossians as the elect of God. This refers to the fact that they had been chosen by God in Christ before the foundation of the world. God's electing grace is one of the mysteries of divine revelation. We believe the Scripture clearly teaches that God, in His sovereignty, had chosen men to belong to Christ. We do not believe that God has ever chosen anyone to be damned. Such a teaching is directly contrary to the Scripture. Just as we believe in God's electing grace, we also believe in man's responsibility. God does not save men against their will. The same Bible that says "elect according to the foreknowledge of God" also says "whosoever shall call upon the name of the Lord shall be saved."

Next Paul addresses the saints as "holy and beloved." "Holy" means sanctified, or set apart to God from the world. We are positionally holy, and we should be practically holy in our lives as well. Because we are the objects of God's love, it hurts Him if we act in an unworthy way. If we are in the consciousness of His love, it gives us a desire to please Him in every way.

Now Paul describes the Christian graces which we are to put on as a garment. "Bowels of mercies" might better be translated "a heart of compassion." The ancients thought of the bowels or intestines as the seat of the emotions. That is why the expression is found so often in the New Testament. "Kindness" speaks of the unselfish spirit of doing for others. It is an attitude of affection or goodwill. "Humbleness of mind" means humility or lowliness. It is the willingness to be abased and to esteem others better than oneself. "Meekness" does not speak of weakness, but rather the strength to deny oneself and to walk in grace toward all men. "The common assumption is that when a man is meek, it is because he cannot help himself; but the Lord was 'meek' because He had the infinite resources of God at His command. Described negatively, meekness is the opposite to self-assertiveness and self-interest; it is equanimity of spirit that is neither elated nor cast down, simply because it is not occupied with self at all"—Vine. If humbleness is "the absence of pride," then meekness is "the absence of passion." "Longsuffering" speaks of patience under provocation and of the long endurance of offense. It combines joyfulness and a kind attitude toward others, along with the endurance of suffering.

"Forbearing one another" describes the attitude of patience **3:13** which we should have with the failings and odd ways of our brethren. In living with others, it is inevitable that we will find out their failures. It often takes the grace of God for us to put up with the idiosyncrasies of others, as it must for them to put up with ours. But we must forbear one another. Not only so, but we must forgive one another, if any man have a quarrel against any. There are few disputes that ever arise among the people of God which could not be quickly solved if these injunctions were heeded. Forgiveness should be exercised toward others when they have offended. We often hear the complaint, "But he was the one who offended me. . . ." That is exactly the type of situation in which we are called upon to forgive. If the other man had not offended us, there would have been no need for forgiveness. If we had been the one who had committed the offense, then we should have gone and asked for pardon. Forbearance suggests our not taking offense; forgiveness not holding it. There could scarcely be any greater incentive to forgiveness than is found in this verse, "Even as Christ forgave you, so also do ye." How did Christ forgive us? He forgave us without a cause. So should we. He forgave us freely. So should we. He forgave and He forgot. So should we. Both as to manner and extent, we should follow our blessed Lord in this wonderful attitude.

Love is here spoken of as the outer garment, or the belt or girdle, **3:14** which binds all the other virtues together in order to make up perfection. It holds together in symmetry all parts of the Christian character. It is possible that a person might manifest some of the virtues above without really having love in his heart. And so Paul is emphasizing here that what we do must be done in a genuine spirit of love for our brethren. Our actions should not be grudging but should be born out of wholehearted affection. The Gnostics thought of knowledge as the bond of perfectness, but Paul corrects this view by insisting that love is the bond.

3:15 The American Standard Version changes the "peace of God" to "the peace of Christ," and most versions agree with this. The thought is that the same peace that characterized the Lord Jesus when He was here and the peace which He imparts to us should act as an umpire in our hearts. If in anything we are in doubt, we should ask ourselves the questions, "Does it make for peace? Or would I have peace in my heart if I went ahead and did it?"

This verse is especially helpful for those seeking guidance from the Lord. If the Lord really wants you to embark upon a certain course of action, He will most assuredly give you peace about it. If you do not have that peace, then you should not proceed. As has often been said, "Darkness about going is light about staying."

Christ called us so that we would enjoy His peace, both as individuals and also in the church. Do not overlook the importance of the latter part of this verse: "To the which ye are called *in one body.*" One way in which we could enjoy peace would be to live in splendid isolation from all other Christians. But this is not God's purpose. He has set the solitary in families. God's intention is that we should gather together in local churches. Although living with other Christians may try our patience at times, yet God in this way can develop virtues in the Christian's life which He could not produce in any other manner. So we should not shirk our responsibilities in the local church, nor give them up when we are annoyed or provoked. Rather we should seek to live compatibly with our fellow-believers and help them in all that we do and say.

"And be ye thankful." You will notice that this refrain is repeated over and over again in Paul's writings. This being so, there must have been a good reason. The Spirit of God must indeed consider a thankful spirit to be very important. And we believe that it is important— important not only for a person's spiritual life, but for his physical welfare as well. Doctors have found out recently what the Scriptures have taught down through the years, that a cheerful, thankful attitude of mind is beneficial for the body, and that worry, depression, and a complaining spirit are definitely harmful to one's health. Usually we think of thankfulness as something that is determined by our immediate circumstances, but Paul here shows that it is a grace to be cultivated. We are responsible to be thankful. Of all peoples of the world, we have the most for which to give thanks (compare Deuteronomy 33:29). The fault is not in any lack of subject matter, but only in our selfish hearts.

3:16

There is considerable disagreement among Bible teachers as to the manner in which verse 16 should be punctuated. Of course, there was no punctuation in the original language of the New Testament, and the meaning of such a verse as this is largely determined by the punctuation marks that are used. We should like to suggest the following: "Let the word of Christ dwell in you richly; in all wisdom teaching and admonishing one another; with psalms and hymns and spiritual songs, singing with grace in your hearts unto God."

According to this version, there are three sections to the verse. First of all, we are to let the word of Christ dwell in us richly. The "word of Christ" refers to the teachings of Christ as found within the covers of the Bible. As we saturate our hearts and minds with His holy Word, and seek to walk in obedience to it, then the word of Christ is really at home in our hearts.

The second thought is that in all wisdom we should teach and admonish one another. Every Christian has a responsibility to his brother in Christ concerning this matter. Teaching has to do with doctrine, whereas admonishing has to do with duty. We owe it to our brethren to share our knowledge of the Scriptures with them, and to seek to help by practical and godly counsel. When teaching and admonition are given in *wisdom*, they are more likely to find acceptance than when we speak with force but unwisely or without love.

The third thing is that with psalms and hymns and spiritual songs we should sing with grace in our hearts unto God. "Psalms" perhaps describe those inspired utterances which are found in the book by that name, which are believed to have been sung as part of Israel's worship. Hymns, on the other hand, might be understood as songs of worship and praise addressed to God the Father or to the Lord Jesus Christ.

141

For example—

> "Jesus! the very thought of Thee
> With sweetness fills my breast;
> But sweeter far Thy face to see,
> And in Thy presence rest."

These hymns would not be inspired in the same sense as the psalms. "Spiritual songs" would refer to religious poetry describing Christian experience. An illustration of this might be found in the words—

> "O what peace we often forfeit,
> O what needless pain we bear,
> All because we do not carry
> Everything to God in prayer."

Using these various types of songs we should sing with grace, or thanksgiving, in our hearts to the Lord. At this point it might be well to say that the Christian should use discernment in the type of music he uses. Much of the so-called Christian music of today is light and frothy. A great deal of this music is utterly contrary to Scripture, and still more is so similar to the jazz and syncopation of the world that it is a dis-credit to the Name of Christ.

Before leaving verse 16, we should notice that it is very similar to Ephesians 5:18, 19. In the latter passage we read: "And be not drunk with wine, wherein is excess; but be filled with the Spirit; Speaking to yourselves in psalms and hymns and spiritual songs, singing and making melody in your heart to the Lord." In Colossians 3:16, the main difference is that instead of saying "be filled with the Spirit," Paul says, "Let the word of Christ dwell in you richly." In other words, being filled with the Spirit and being filled with God's Word are both requisites for living joyful, useful, fruitful lives. We shall not be filled with the Spirit unless we are saturated with God's Word; and the study of God's Word will not be effective unless we yield up our inmost being to the control of the Holy Spirit. Can we not therefore conclude that to be filled with the Spirit means to be filled with God's Word? It is not some mysterious, emotional crisis that comes in the life, but rather day by day feeding on the Scriptures, meditating on them, obeying them, and living by them.

Here in verse 17 is an all-inclusive rule by which to judge our conduct as Christians. Young people today especially have a difficult time deciding whether certain things are right or wrong. This verse, committed to memory, might prove to be the key for unlocking many of these problems. The great test should be, "Can I do this in the name of the Lord Jesus Christ? Would this be to His glory? Could I expect His blessing to rest upon it? Would I want to be doing it when He comes back again?" Notice that this test should apply to the words which we speak and to the deeds we do. It has been said that obedience to this command ennobles all life. It is a precious secret when the Christian learns to do all as unto the Lord and for His glory. Once again the apostle adds the word "Giving thanks to God and the Father through Him." Thanks! Thanks! Thanks! It is a perpetual duty for those saved by grace and destined for the courts of heaven.

When you have mastered this lesson, take the first part of Exam 5 (covering lesson 9), questions 1-10 on pages 159-161 (right after lesson 10).

Concluding Advice and Greetings

Colossians 3:18—4:18

IV. Advice to members of the Christian household (3:18—4:1).
   a. Wives and husbands (vv. 18, 19).
   b. Children and parents (vv. 20, 21).
   c. Servants and masters (vv. 22—4:1).

*   *   *

  I. Pray (vv. 2-4).
   a. Stedfastly (v. 2).
   b. Watchfully (v. 2).
   c. Thankfully (v. 2).
   d. Particularly—for Paul (vv. 3, 4).
 II. Walk (v. 5).
   a. Wisely (v. 5).
   b. Opportunely (v. 5).
III. Talk (v. 6).
   a. Graciously (v. 6).
   b. Seasonably (v. 6).
   c. Intelligently (v. 6).
IV. Personal glimpses of Paul's friendships (vv. 7-14).
   a. Tychicus—mailman (vv. 7, 8).
   b. Onesimus—converted runaway-slave (v. 9).
   c. Aristarchus—fellow-prisoner (v. 10).
   d. Mark—writer of the second gospel (v. 10).

THE CHRISTIAN HOUSEHOLD (3:18—4:1)

3:18 With this verse Paul begins a section of exhortations to members of the Christian household. The series continues through verse 1 of chapter 4. Here he has advice for wives and husbands, for children and parents, and for servants and masters.

At first, it may seem like an abrupt change for Paul to turn from the subjects which have occupied him to such mundane matters as home life. But actually this is most significant. It shows conclusively that God considers the home to be a very important force in the Christian life. The well-known statement, "The hand that rocks the cradle rules the world," has truth in it beyond what appears on the surface. The family unit was designed by God for the preservation of much that is worthwhile in life. As less and less attention is devoted to the home, even so our civilization deteriorates rapidly. Paul's first letter to Timothy teaches in a special way that God has ordained home life as the means of developing spiritual qualities, so that one's fitness for leadership in the church grows out of his proved character in the home.

In the verses to follow we have some of the fundamental principles to guide in the establishment of a Christian home. In studying this section, the student should be aware of the following "musts."

1. There must be a family altar—a time each day when the family gathers together for the reading of the Holy Scriptures and for prayer.

2. The father must have his place of authority in the home, and he must exercise it in wisdom and love.

146

3. The wife and mother should realize that her first responsibility to God and to the family is in the home. In general, it is not wise for the wife to have an outside job. There are, of course, exceptional cases.

4. The husband and wife should present a godly example to their children. They should be united on all matters, including the disciplining of the children, when necessary.

5. The family unit should be maintained. It is all too possible to become so engrossed in business, social life, and even in Christian service that the children suffer from lack of affection, companionship, instruction, and discipline. Many parents have had to confess mournfully over a wayward son or daughter: "As thy servant was busy here and there, he was gone" (1 Kings 20:40).

6. With regard to the disciplining of children, three cardinal rules have been suggested. Never punish in anger. Never punish unjustly. Never punish without explaining the reason.

7. It is good for children to learn to bear the yoke in their youth (Lamentations 3:27), to learn the discipline of work and of accepting responsibility, and the value of a dollar.

8. Above all, Christian parents should avoid being ambitious for their children in a carnal, worldly way, but should constantly hold before them the service of our Lord as the most profitable way in which to spend their lives. For some, it might mean full-time service on a mission field; for others, it might mean service for the Lord in a secular occupation. But in either case, work for the Lord should be the primary consideration. Whether at home, at work, or wherever we may be, we should be conscious of the fact that we represent our Savior, and so every word and act should be worthy of Him, and should, in fact, be governed by Him.

In verse 18, the first injunction of the apostle is addressed to wives. They are enjoined to submit themselves to their own husbands, as is fit in the Lord. According to the divine plan, the husband is head of the house. The woman has been given the place of subjection to her husband. She is not to dominate or to lead, but to follow his leadership, wherever she can do so without compromising her loyalty to Christ.

There are, of course, instances in which the woman cannot obey her husband and still be faithful to Christ. In such an instance, of course, her first loyalty is to the Lord Jesus. Where a Christian woman has a backward husband, this verse indicates that she should help him to fulfil his proper place in the home, rather than for her to usurp it because she may be more clever.

3:19   The balance which is presented to us in the Word of God is beautiful. The apostle does not stop with this advice to wives; he now goes on to show that husbands, too, have a responsibility. They are to love their wives, and not to be bitter against them. If these simple precepts were followed today, many of the problems of married life would disappear, and homes would be happier in the Lord. Actually no wife would be likely to object to submitting herself to a husband who truly loves her. It has been noted that the husband is not told to make his wife obey him. If she does not, he should take it to the Lord. The submission should be her voluntary act "as unto the Lord."

3:20   Children are admonished to "obey their parents in all things: for this is well-pleasing unto the Lord." It has been well said that in all ages, families have been held together by two simple principles—authority and obedience. Here we have the latter. Notice too that this obedience is to be in all things. This means not only in the things that are agreeable, but those which are not so naturally pleasing.

Christian children who have unsaved parents are often placed in a difficult position. They want to be true to the Lord, and yet at the same time they are faced with demands made upon them by their parents. In general we feel that if they honor their parents, God will in turn honor them. As long as they are living in the home of their parents, they have a very definite obligation to perform. Of course, they should not do anything that would be contrary to the teachings of Christ, but ordinarily they would not be called upon to do such. Oftentimes they will be called upon to do things that might seem very distasteful to them, but as long as it is not distinctly wrong or sinful, they can determine to do it as unto the Lord. In this way they can be a good testimony to their parents and seek to win them to the Lord.

3:21   Fathers should not provoke their children, lest they should become discouraged. It is interesting that this advice is addressed to fathers and not to mothers. Does it not reveal that the danger of a father committing this fault is greater than that of a mother? Some commentators tell us that the word "fathers" here should really be "parents." In that case, the counsel would be applicable to both fathers and mothers, and undoubtedly it is. However, it still remains true that fathers are probably the chief offenders in this regard. Kelly suggests that mothers are probably more prone to spoil the children.

From verse 22 to the end of the chapter, the spirit of God **3:22** addresses servants or slaves. It is interesting to note the amount of space devoted in the New Testament to slaves. This is not without significance. It shows that no matter how low a person's social status in life may be, he still can attain the very highest in the Christian life through faithfulness to the Word of God. Perhaps it also reflects the foreknowledge of God that most Christian people would occupy places of service rather than positions of authority. For instance, there is very little instruction in the New Testament that refers to rulers of nations, but there is considerable advice for those who devote their lives in the service of others. Slaves in the days of Paul usually received very little consideration, and doubtless it struck the early Christians as unusual that so much attention was given to them in these letters. But it shows how the grace of God reaches down to men, no matter how menial their position might be. "The slave is not shut out from the service of God. By simply doing his duty in the sight of God, he can adorn the doctrine and bring glory to God"—C. H. Mackintosh.

Servants are told to obey in all things those who are their masters according to the flesh. There is a gentle reminder here that these masters are only masters according to the flesh. They have another Master Who is above all and Who sees all that is done to the lowliest of His children. Slaves are not to serve with eye-service, as menpleasers, but in singleness of heart, fearing the Lord. (For a good example of this in the Old Testament, see Genesis 24:33.) Especially when a person is oppressed, it is a temptation to slack off in his work when the master is not looking. But the Christian servant will realize that his Master is always looking, and so even though his earthly circumstances may be very bitter, he will work as unto the Lord. "In singleness of heart" means that he will have a pure motive—only to please the Lord Jesus.

While speaking on the subject of slaves, it is interesting to notice that there is no express prohibition against slavery in the New Testament. The Gospel does not overthrow social institutions by revolution. However, wherever the Gospel has gone, slavery has been uprooted and eliminated. This does not mean that these instructions are therefore without meaning. All that is said here may very well be applied to employees and employers.

3:23 Whatever is done should be done heartily (from the soul—Vincent) as to the Lord and not unto men. In every form of Christian service as well as in every sphere of life, there are many tasks which people find to be obnoxious. Needless to say, we try to avoid such work. But this verse teaches us the very important lesson that the humblest service can be glorified and dignified by doing it for the Lord. In this sense, there is no difference between secular and sacred work. All is sacred. Rewards in heaven will not be according to how pleasant our work was or how spectacular; they will not be for prominence or apparent successes; they will not be for talents or opportunities; but rather for faithfulness. Thus obscure persons will fare very well in that day if they have carried out their duties faithfully as unto the Lord. Two mottoes which are often hung over the kitchen sink are: "Not somehow, but triumphantly," and "Divine service held here three times daily."

3:24 The Lord is keeping the records at the present time, and everything done as unto Him will command His attention. "The kindness of God will repay the kindness of men." Those who have little of earthly inheritance will receive the recompense of the inheritance in heaven. Let us remember this the next time we are called upon to do something that we do not like to do, whether in the local assembly, in the home, or at work; it is a testimony for Christ to do it uncomplainingly, and to do the best possible job.

3:25 Paul does not specify just whom he has in mind in verse 25. Perhaps we would most naturally think of an unjust master, one who oppresses his servants. Maybe a Christian servant has become weary of obeying his unjust demands. "Never mind," Paul is saying, "the Lord knows all about it, and He will take care of the wrongs, too."

But although this might include masters, it is addressed primarily to servants. Slipshod service, cheating, loafing, or other forms of insincerity will not go unnoticed. There is no respect of persons with God. He is the Master of all, and the distinctions that prevail among men mean nothing to Him. If slaves rob their masters (as did Onesimus), they will have to give an account to the Lord.

This verse rightly belongs with the closing verses of chapter three. **4:1** Masters should render unto their servants that which is just and equal. They should not withhold from them a proper wage, but should pay them well for the work which they have done. This is addressed directly to Christian employers. God hates the oppression of the poor, and the gifts of a man who has grown rich through unfair labor practices are unacceptable to the Lord. God says in effect, "You keep your money; I don't like the way you made it" (see James 5:1-4). Masters should not be high-minded but should fear. They also have a Master in heaven, One who is just and righteous in all His ways.

Before closing this section it is interesting to note how the apostle Paul repeatedly brings these matters of everyday life under the searchlight of the Lordship of Christ. C. R. Erdman has shown this emphasis as follows: (1) Wives—as is fitting in the Lord (v. 18). (2) Children—well-pleasing to the Lord (v. 20). (3) Servants—fearing the Lord (A.S.V., v. 22). (4) Servants—as to the Lord (v. 23).

CHRISTIAN LIVING (4:2-6)

The apostle never tires of exhorting the people of God to be diligent in **4:2** their prayer life. Doubtless one of the regrets we all will have when we get to heaven will be that we did not spend more time in prayer, especially when we will realize the extent to which our prayers were answered. There is a great deal of mystery in connection with the whole subject of prayer. There are many questions which cannot be answered. But the best attitude for the Christian is not to seek to analyze prayer, to dissect it, to understand its deeper mysteries. The best approach is to continue to pray in simple faith, leaving aside one's intellectual doubts.

Not only are we to continue in prayer, but we are also to watch in the same. This immediately reminds us of the Lord Jesus' request to the disciples in the Garden of Gethsemane, "Watch and pray, that ye enter not into temptation." They did not watch, and so fell sound asleep. Not only are we to watch against sleep, but also against wandering thoughts, against listlessness, and against unreality. And we are to watch to see that we are not robbed of time for prayer (Ephesians 6: 18). Then again, our prayers are to be with thanksgiving. Not only are we to be thankful for past answers to prayer, but in faith we can also thank the Lord for prayers that He has not answered. We know that "His love wants the best for us; His wisdom knows the best for us; and His power gets the best for us"—Guy King.

4:3 Paul asks that the Colossians remember to pray for him also, and for the servants of the Lord who are with him in Rome. It is beautiful to notice that he does not ask that he might be released from prison, but rather that God may open the door to him for preaching the Word. The apostle wanted God to open doors for him. What an important lesson there is for us in this! It is all too possible for us to go around opening doors for ourselves in Christian service. But this is a peril to be avoided. If the Lord opens the doors to us, then we can confidently enter them, knowing that He is leading. On the other hand, if we open the doors for ourselves, then we cannot be sure that we are in the center of the Lord's will, and we might soon be stooping to carnal means to carry on the so-called work of the Lord. Paul's specific request is that a door of utterance might be opened to him to speak the mystery of Christ, for which he was in bonds. The mystery of Christ in this verse is the truth of the Church, and particularly that aspect of it which might be defined by the expression "Christ for the Gentiles." That was the special aspect of the gospel message which had been committed to Paul to preach. It was because he dared to suggest that Gentiles could be saved in the same way as Jews that the Jewish people finally succeeded in having him sent to Rome as a prisoner.

There are some Christians who teach that the great mystery of the Church was revealed to Paul while he was in prison. They therefore put great emphasis on the "Prison Epistles" while seeming to underestimate the importance of the Gospel and other books of the New Testament. But it is clear from this verse that the preaching of the mystery was the *cause* of his imprisonment and therefore must have been revealed to him some time before his arrest.

He is anxious to make it manifest, that is, to preach it in such a **4:4** clear manner that it will be readily understood by the people. This should be the desire of every Christian as he seeks to make Christ known. There is no virtue in being deep. We should aim to reach the masses of humanity and, in order to do so, the message must be presented simply and clearly.

Christians should walk in wisdom toward them that are without. **4:5** In their everyday behavior, they should realize that they are being carefully watched by unbelievers. The world is more interested in our walk than in our talk. Men say, in the language of Edgar Guest, "I'd rather see a sermon, than hear one, any day." This does not mean that the Christian should not also confess Christ with his lips, but the point is that his walk should correspond with his talk. It should never be said of him, "High talk, low walk."

"Redeeming the time." Literally, this means "buying up opportunities." Every day of our lives we face opportunities for witnessing to the saving power of the Lord Jesus Christ. As these opportunities come along, we should be ready to snap them up. The word "buying" implies that there is often a cost involved. But whatever the cost may be, we should be ready to share our precious Savior with those who do not know Him.

Our conversation should be always with grace, seasoned with salt, **4:6** that we might know how to answer every man. If our speech is to be always with grace, it must be courteous, humble, and Christ-like. It should be free from gossip, frivolity, uncleanness, and bitterness. The expression "seasoned with salt" may have several different meanings. Some commentators think that although our language should be gracious, it should be equally honest and without hypocrisy. Others think of salt as that which heightens flavor, and so they feel that Paul is saying that our conversation should never be dull, flat, or insipid, but should always be worthwhile and profitable. Lightfoot says that heathen writers used "salt" as a figure of speech for "wit." Paul changes wit to wisdom. Perhaps the best way to explain the expression is to study the language of the Lord Jesus. To the woman taken in the act of adultery, He said, "Neither do I condemn thee: go, and sin no more." Here we have the grace and the salt. First of all, the grace, "neither do I condemn thee"; then the salt, "go, and sin no more." Then again the Lord Jesus said to the woman at Jacob's well, "Give me to drink . . . Go, call thy husband." The first speaks of grace, whereas the second reminds us more of salt.

"That ye may know how to answer every man." Perhaps the apostle Paul is here thinking particularly of the Gnostics who came to the Colossians with their plausible doctrines. They should be ready to answer these false teachers with words of wisdom and faithfulness.

SOME OF PAUL'S FRIENDS (4:7-14)

4:7 *Tychicus* was apparently the one who was chosen by the apostle Paul to carry this letter from Rome to Colosse. Maclaren pictures how amazed Tychicus would have been if told that "these bits of parchment would outlast all the ostentatious pomp of the city, and that his name, because written in them, would be known to the end of time all over the world."

Paul here assures the saints that when Tychicus arrives he will give them a full account of the apostle's affairs.

Again it is nice to read the combination of titles which Paul bestows on this brother. He calls him "a beloved brother, a faithful minister and fellowservant in the Lord." How much more to be coveted are titles such as these than high-sounding ecclesiastical names that are given to church officials in our day.

4:8 Tychicus' trip to Colosse would serve two purposes. First of all, he would give the saints a firsthand account of Paul and his companions in Rome, and also he would comfort the hearts of the Colossians. Here again, "to comfort" has more the idea of "to strengthen" or "to confirm" than that of "to console." His ministry to them would have the general effect of helping them to stand against the false teaching that was then prevalent.

4:9 The mention of the name *Onesimus* brings before us the lovely story that is unfolded in Paul's letter to Philemon. Onesimus was the slave who had run away from Philemon and had sought to escape from

154

punishment by fleeing to Rome. In some way, however, he had come in contact with the apostle Paul, and Paul, in turn, had pointed the runaway slave to the Lord Jesus Christ. Now Onesimus is going to travel back to his former master, Philemon, in Colosse. He will carry Paul's letter to Philemon, while Tychicus carries the letter to the church at Colosse. Can you not picture the excitement among the believers in Colosse when these two brethren arrived with the letters from Paul? Doubtless they all sat up very late in the evening, asking questions about conditions in Rome and hearing of Paul's indomitable courage in the service of his Savior.

Not much is known about *Aristarchus* except that he had prev- 4:10 iously been arrested in connection with his service for the Lord, as is recorded in Acts 19:29. Now he is in prison with Paul in Rome.

Mark is here spoken of as Barnabas' sister's son. However, the correct translation is that Mark was a cousin of Barnabas rather than a nephew. You will remember the story of how this young man had started out with Paul and Barnabas in missionary labors. Because of his failure, Paul decided that he should be left at home, but Barnabas insisted on taking him with him. This caused a rift between the two elder workers. However, it is nice to learn that Mark's failure was not final, and he is now restored to the confidence of the beloved Paul.

If Mark should visit Colosse, the saints there are told to receive him. The expression "touching whom ye received commandments" does not necessarily mean that the Colossians had previously received instructions concerning Mark. It more probably refers to the instructions which Paul is now giving to them: "If he come unto you, receive him." The tense of the verb "received" may simply mean that by the time the Colossians read this letter, they would have received instructions. The mention of Mark as a gospel writer reminds us that we are all writing a gospel day by day:

"We each write a gospel, a chapter a day,
By deeds, looks and likes, the things that we say,
Our actions betray us—words faithful and true—
Say, 'What is the gospel according to you?' "

Another co-worker of Paul is spoken of as "Jesus, which is called 4:11

155

Justus." Jesus was a common name then, as it still is in certain countries. It was the Greek equivalent of the Hebrew name "Joshua." No doubt this man was called Justus because his Christian friends would feel the incongruity of anyone having the same name as the Son of God.

The three foregoing men were all converted Jews. Indeed they were the only three former Jews who were co-workers with Paul in the kingdom of God, men who had been a help to him.

4:12 As Paul is bringing his letter to a close, *Epaphras* reminds him to be sure to send his own personal greetings to the dear saints in Colosse. Epaphras, as you will remember, was a native of Colosse, and he was constantly remembering the believers in his prayers, asking the Lord that they might stand perfect and fully assured in all the will of God.

4:13 Paul bears witness to the fact that Epaphras travailed in prayer not only for those in Colosse, but also for the Christians in Laodicea and in Hierapolis. This man had a personal interest in the people of God with whom he was acquainted. Doubtless he had a very long prayer list, and it would not be at all surprising if he remembered each one in prayer every day. (The writer has personally been acquainted with elders in local churches who made it a point to mention the names of those in their local church every day at the throne of grace.)

4:14 Now Paul sends greetings from *Luke,* the beloved physician, and Demas. Here we have a study in contrasts. Luke had traveled with Paul considerably and had probably ministered to him both physically and spiritually during his times of sickness, persecution, and imprisonment.

Demas, on the other hand, had gone on with the apostle for a while, but it was necessary for the apostle to say of him eventually, "Demas hath forsaken me, having loved this present world, and is departed unto Thessalonica" (2 Timothy 4:10).

4:15 **PERSONAL GREETINGS** (4:15-18)

Greetings are now sent to the brethren that are in Laodicea, to *Nymphas,* and to the church that was in his house. We read again of the church in Laodicea in Revelation 3:14-22. The church there became lukewarm about the things of God. It became utterly materialistic and self-satisfied. Thinking that all was well, the people did not realize their own nakedness. Bible teachers are not clear whether Nymphas was a man or a woman. But it is sufficient to notice that there was a church in that home in Colosse. In those days, of course, the Christians did not have elaborate edifices such as are used today. However, most of us will readily agree that the power of God in a local church is far more important than an elaborate building or fine furnishings. Power is not dependent upon the latter, but luxurious church buildings often serve as a hindrance to power.

After this letter had been read in Colosse, it was to be sent to the church in Laodicea to be read there also. Undoubtedly this was done, but from what we learn in Revelation 3, it seems obvious that the Laodiceans did not heed the message of this epistle. **4:16**

Paul also directs that the letter from Laodicea should be read in Colosse. There is no definite way of knowing just what letter is referred to. Some believe that Paul's so-called letter to the Ephesians was the one in view. Actually, some ancient authorities omit the words "at Ephesus" in Ephesians 1:1. This has led commentators to believe that the letter to the Ephesians might have been a circular letter which was supposed to be read in several different churches—for instance, Ephesus, Laodicea, then Colosse. This view is also strengthened by the fact that so few personal references are made in Ephesians in comparison to the number made in the letter to the Colossians.

Archippus is told to take heed to the ministry which he had received in the Lord, and to fulfil it. Here again, we do not have definite information as to what ministry is referred to. Many have believed that Archippus was a son of Philemon, and that he was active in the church at Colosse. The verse will become much more meaningful to us if we assume that our name is Archippus, and if we hear the Spirit of God saying to us, "Take heed to the ministry which thou hast received in the Lord, that thou fulfil it." Each one of us has been given some service by the Lord, and we will some day be required to give an account of what we have done with it. **4:17**

At this point, the apostle Paul took the pen in his own hand and signed his closing salutation. Doubtless as he did so the chain around his right hand proved an inconvenience in writing, but it reminded him **4:18**

to say to the Colossians, "Remember my bonds." "The sound of pen
and chains together is the final sign that the preacher's chains cannot
bind the Word of God"—*New Bible Commentary.* Then he closed the
epistle with the words "Grace be with you." "There is no richer word
than the word 'grace,' for it carries in it all of God's love as seen in the
gift of His Son for us"—A. T. Robertson.

When you are ready, complete Exam 5 by answering questions
11-20 on pages 161-164. (You should have already answered
questions 1-10 as part of your study of lesson 9.)

PHILIPPIANS, COLOSSIANS and PHILEMON   *Exam 5*
                                                    Lessons 9, 10

Exam
Name_____ Grade_____
                    (print plainly)
Address _____
                                    Zip   Class
City_____ State _____ Code _____ Number _____

Instructor _____

LESSON 9

In the blank space in the right-hand margin write the letter of the correct answer.
(50 points)

1. When Paul says "If then ye were raised together with Christ,
    . . ." the "if"
    a. is foreign to the original text and has crept into the trans-
       lation through error
    b. means that some Christians do not attain to the experience
       he is describing
    c. could better be translated as "since"
    d. ought to be underlined in our thinking because it is the
       most important word in the passage   _____

2. The counterpart of our death with Christ is our
    a. baptism with the Holy Spirit
    b. conflict with the lusts of the flesh
    c. complete deliverance from the possibility of further tempta-
       tion
    d. identification with Christ in resurrection   _____

3. The expression "your life is hid with Christ in God" means
    a. we ought to be occupied with things which are bound up
       in Christ
    b. the believer's spiritual life is unseen by the world which, as
       a result, does not understand him
    c. both the above
    d. neither of the above but rather that our salvation should be
       kept hidden from men   _____

4. The Biblical attitude towards sex is that it
a. is taboo as a subject of discussion
b. is beautiful and ought to be given free expression
c. must be kept in its proper place and regulated by the dictates of holiness
d. is inherently sinful and should be repressed _____

5. Immorality is something which
a. men can indulge with impunity
b. is always visited by God with immediate judgment
c. incurs God's displeasure but not His wrath
d. invariably results, sooner or later in judgment from God _____

6. Paul warned the Colossians against
a. sins of the disposition such as anger and malice but not against sins of the tongue
b. sins of the tongue such as blasphemy, filthy conversation and lying but not against such sins as fornication
c. sins of the body, the tongue and disposition
d. blasphemy against the Holy Ghost which is the unpardonable sin _____

7. Paul's expression "the old man"
a. is a slang reference to one's natural father
b. has to do with "the man of old," the man we used to be before we were saved
c. refers primarily to Adam
d. is a reference to senior members of the Christian community _____

8. One thing Paul does **NOT** recommend we "put on" as Christians is
a. a heart of compassion
b. an attitude of affection and goodwill
c. a willingness to be abased
d. a spirit of weakness
e. self-denial
f. patience under provocation _____

9. The expression "the peace of God" in Colossians 3:15 is better translated—
a. "peace with God"
b. "the peace of Christ"
c. "a lack of hostility Godward"
d. "a peace from God" _____

10. Putting Colossians 3:16 together with Ephesians 5:18, 19, we conclude that
    a. the baptism of the Spirit is a kind of "second blessing" towards which all believers should strive
    b. the Bible becomes the Word of God to us only as we read and obey it
    c. being filled with the Spirit depends to a large extent on being filled with God's Word
    d. psalms, hymns and spiritual songs are all equally inspired by the Holy Spirit _____

WHAT DO YOU SAY?

What practical result has the study of this lesson had in your own life?

_____

_____

_____

_____

_____

LESSON 10

In the blank space in the right-hand margin write the letter of the correct answer. (45 points)

11. The woman's place in the home is to
    a. be in subjection to her husband in all things even if it involves disloyalty at times to the Lord
    b. follow the leadership of her husband except where it means compromising loyalty to the Lord
    c. accept the place of leadership in the family only if she is clever and more aggressive by nature than her husband
    d. enjoy complete "woman's liberation" and assume equality with her husband in the leadership role _____

12. Children must
    a. be given complete equality with parents in deciding their role as children in the family circle
    b. obey their parents always and in everything even when it involves doing things which are actually sinful
    c. submit to their parents as unto the Lord
    d. be allowed freedom to refuse to do things which displease them since any attempt to force obedience violates their rights as human beings and gives them inhibitions _____

13. Paul's word to slaves was that they
    a. organize against the repressive establishment which upheld slavery
    b. engage in mass demonstrations so as to secure their civil rights
    c. protest the injustices done to them by society by engaging in civil disobedience and passive resistance
    d. obey their masters in all things
    e. pray for their freedom

14. In employer-employee relations, Paul
    a. advocated the formation of unions to insure that employees receive proper treatment
    b. endorsed the "go slow" principle as just and fair in cases where employers fail to give proper remuneration for work done
    c. told employers to give their employees just and proper working conditions
    d. was the first to suggest to workers that they strike for higher wages _____

15. We learn from Colossians that
    a. the prison epistles are of special importance because the great mystery of the Church was revealed to Paul while he was in prison
    b. Paul was in prison because he was preaching the great mystery of the Church
    c. Paul's experience in prison had taught him to be more cautious in proclaiming the mystery
    d. the prison epistles were actually the first of the Pauline letters to be written _____

16. Tychicus was
   a. a fellow prisoner of Paul in Rome
   b. a slave in Caesar's household
   c. a beloved brother of Paul and a faithful servant of the Lord
   d. an ordained bishop in the church at Rome   ————

17. **Which of the following was in prison with Paul at Rome?**
   a. **Aristarchus**
   b. **Mark**
   c. **Onesimus**
   d. **Timothy**   ————

18. Paul told the Colossians that
   a. Demas had forsaken him
   b. Nymphas would be arriving in Colosse soon with further
      news from Rome
   c. Epaphras was praying for them
   d. Justus was teaching false doctrine   ————

19. The final warning in Colossians is
   a. to make sure to fulfil one's ministry
   b. to beware of legalism
   c. to avoid fellowship with false teachers
   d. to remember the Judgment Seat of Christ   ————

20. Picture the following situation. A young believer with good prospects of promotion in the company for which he works is called into his employer's office.

"John," says the employer, "If Mr. Brown comes in today I don't want to see him. I'm going to be busy all day getting these accounts cleared up. You know what Sam Brown is like—talk! talk! talk! I'll never get anything done once he gets in here. At the same time I can't afford to offend him; he's our best customer. You tell him I'm out."

Suggest an answer of grace, seasoned with salt, you might give your employer if you were John. *(5 points)*

————————————————————————

————————————————————————

————————————————————————

————————————————————————

————————————————————————

163

WHAT DO YOU SAY?

How are you practicing the principles of Scripture regarding the home as these principles apply to you?

_____

_____

_____

_____

_____

Lesson Eleven

Praise for Philemon

Philemon 1-7

I. Salutation (1-3).
II. Paul's Thanksgiving and Prayer for Philemon (4-7).

INTRODUCTION

We have to piece together the story behind this letter from the contents of the epistle itself and from Paul's letter to the Colossians. It appears that Philemon was a resident of Colosse (compare Colossians 4:17 with Philemon 2) who had been converted through the apostle Paul (v. 19). One of his slaves or servants, Onesimus, had run away from him (vv. 15, 16) and there is a hint that Onesimus might have helped himself to some of his master's possessions as well (v. 18).

The fugitive reached Rome at the time that Paul was imprisoned there (v. 9). We cannot be sure whether the apostle was actually behind bars at the time or whether it was during the period when he was allowed the freedom of his own hired house (Acts 28:30). By a curious chain of circumstances, Onesimus met Paul in the busy metropolis and was led to Christ through his ministry (v. 10). In the days that followed, a mutual bond of love developed (v. 12) and Onesimus proved to be a valued helper to the apostle (v. 13). But they both agreed that the proper thing would be for Onesimus to return to Philemon and make right the wrongs of the past. So Paul wrote this letter to Philemon,

165

interceding for Onesimus and presenting strong reasons why he should be graciously restored to his master's favor (v. 17). It was at this time that Paul also wrote the letter to the Colossians. He assigned Tychicus to act as mailman and sent Onesimus back with him (Colossians 4:7-9).

When was the letter written? Probably about thirty years after the death of Christ. This is the most personal of all Paul's letters. The epistles to Timothy and Titus were also written to individuals but they deal with matters of assembly practice more than with personal affairs.

SALUTATION (1-3)

v. 1 Paul introduces himself as a prisoner rather than an apostle. He could have used his authority, but he prefers to appeal from what might seem a low place of disadvantage. Yet the apostle gilds this low place with the glory of heaven. He is a "prisoner of Jesus Christ." Not for a minute will he grovel as a prisoner of Rome. He sees beyond the emperor to the King of kings. Timothy was with him as he wrote, and so he links this faithful disciple with him, though the letter is obviously Paul's.

The main addressee is Philemon. His name means "affectionate" and apparently he was true to the name because Paul describes him as **v. 2** "our dearly beloved and fellow-labourer." Since Apphia is a feminine name, most Bible teachers assume that she was Mrs. Philemon. The fact that the letter is addressed to her, in part, reminds us that Christianity exalts womanhood. Later we shall see how it also exalts slaves. Sanctified imagination has almost invariably identified Archippus as the son of Philemon. We can't be sure, but we do know that he was actively engaged in the Christian warfare. Paul honors him as a fellow-soldier. We can picture him as a dedicated, devoted disciple of the Lord Jesus, on fire with a holy passion. In the letter to the Colossians, Paul singled him out for special attention: "And say to Archippus, Take heed to the ministry which thou hast received in the Lord, that thou fulfil it" (Colossians 4:17).

If the mention of Philemon, Apphia and Archippus give us a picture of a New Testament Christian family, the expression, ". . . and to the church in thy house," calls up the image of a New Testament church. It seems clear from this that Philemon's house was the meeting place for an assembly of believers. It was there they gathered for worship, prayer and Bible study. From there they went forth to witness for Christ in a world that would never welcome their message but would never forget it either.

As they met together in Philemon's home, the Christians were all one in Christ Jesus. Rich and poor, male and female, master and slave—all were there as full-fledged members of the family of God. As soon as they returned to the work-a-day world, their social distinctions would reappear. But at the Lord's Supper, for instance, they were all on the common level of holy priests. Philemon would have no precedence over Onesimus.

v. 3 Paul's characteristic greeting seems to embody the best he could desire for those he loved. Grace includes all the undeserved favor which God showers on His people. Peace here is the spiritual serenity and poise which stabilize the lives of those who are taught by His grace. Both blessings come from God our Father and the Lord Jesus Christ. This is full of significance. It means that the Lord Jesus is equal with God the Father in bestowing grace and peace. It would be blasphemy to give such honor to Christ if He were not truly and fully God.

PAUL'S PRAISE AND PRAYER FOR PHILEMON (4-7)

v. 4 Whenever the apostle prayed for Philemon, he thanked God for this noble brother. We have every reason to believe that he was a choice trophy of the grace of God—the kind of man you like to have as a friend and brother. Some commentators suggest that Paul is using diplomacy in these opening verses, that his purpose is to "soften" Philemon's heart to receive Onesimus back again. This ascribes an unworthy motive to the apostle and casts an unfavorable shadow over the inspired text. Paul would not have said it if he had not sincerely meant it.

v. 5 There were two qualities in the character of Philemon that gave great joy to Paul—his love and the faith which he had toward the Lord

Jesus and all the saints. His faith in Christ showed he had the root of divine life and his love toward all the saints showed that he had the fruit as well. His faith was productive.

In Ephesians 1:15 and Colossians 1:4, Paul had expressed similar thanks for the saints to whom those letters were addressed. However, in those two places he put faith before love. Here he puts love before faith. Why the difference? Maclaren answers: "The order here is the order of analysis, digging down from manifestation to cause. The order in the parallel passages is the order of production ascending from root to flower."

There is another interesting feature of Paul's arrangement here. He divides the expression "Love toward all saints" by inserting "faith . . . toward the Lord Jesus" after love. We might put it as follows: "love (and faith . . . toward the Lord Jesus) toward all saints." The object of faith is the Lord Jesus. The object of love is the saints. But Paul wraps the faith clause with the love clause, as if to forewarn Philemon that he is about to have a special opportunity to manifest the reality of his faith by showing love to the slave Onesimus. Thus there is special emphasis in the word *all—all* the saints.

v. 6 The previous two verses expressed Paul's thanks for Philemon. This one discloses the nature of the apostle's prayer for him. The wording in the King James Version is admittedly difficult. As is often the case, the American Standard Version comes to our rescue with this simpler translation: "And I pray that the sharing of your faith may promote the knowledge of all the good that is ours in Christ."

The *sharing of his faith* means the practical kindness which Philemon showed to others. We can share our faith not only by preaching Christ but also by feeding the hungry, clothing the destitute, comforting the bereaved, relieving the distressed—yes, even by forgiving a runaway slave. Paul prayed then that Philemon's life of benevolence would lead many to a full knowledge of all the good things that belong to those who are members of Christ. There is tremendous power and influence in a life where the love of God is manifest. It is one thing to read about love in a book, but how compelling it is to see the Word become flesh in a human life.

v. 7 News of Philemon's overflowing generosity and self-sacrificial love traveled from Colosse to Rome, bringing cheer and comfort to Christ's prisoner. It had been a great privilege for Paul to lead Philemon to the Lord, but now how rewarding it was to hear that his child in the faith was going on well for the Lord. How assuring it was to know that the hearts of the saints were being greatly refreshed by this beloved brother, and especially by his love. No one lives to himself, and no one dies to himself. Our actions affect others. We cannot measure the range of our influence. We have limitless potential for good or for evil.

When you have mastered this lesson, take the first part of Exam 6 (covering lesson 11), questions 1-10 on pages179-180(right after lesson 12).

The Plea for Onesimus

Philemon 8-25

I.   Paul's plea for Onesimus (8-20).
II. Closing Remarks (21-25).

THE PLEA FOR ONESIMUS (8-20)

Now the apostle comes to the main purpose of the letter. He is about **v. 8** to intercede for Onesimus. But how will he approach the subject? As an apostle, he could justifiably say to Philemon, "Now, my brother, it is your duty as a believer to forgive and restore this runaway, and that's exactly what I'm telling you to do." Paul could have ordered him to do it, and Philemon would no doubt have obeyed. But that would have been a hollow victory in this case.

If the apostle did not win Philemon's heart, then Onesimus might **v. 9** have returned to an icy reception. Only obedience that was motivated by love would make the slave's status in the home tolerable. Perhaps as he wrote this, Paul thought of the Savior's words, "If ye love me, keep my commandments" (John 14:15). And so for love's sake, he preferred to appeal rather than to order. Would Philemon's love reach across the sea where an aged ambassador of Christ was a prisoner for the Lord Jesus?

Would he be moved by two considerations—Paul, the *aged* and now a *prisoner?* We do not know exactly how old the apostle was at

171

this time. Estimates range from fifty-three to sixty-three. That might not seem old to us today, but he was probably prematurely old because of the way he had burnt himself out in the service of Christ.

And now he was a prisoner for Christ Jesus. In mentioning this, he wasn't looking for sympathy, but he did hope that Philemon would weigh these factors in making his decision. Some versions translate *Paul, an ambassador* rather than *Paul, the aged.* Either thought is acceptable, though the latter seems more likely to reach Philemon's heart.

v. 10 In the original of this verse the name *Onesimus* comes last. "I entreat thee concerning a son of mine, whom I have begotten in my bonds—Onesimus" (Barnes). By the time Philemon reached the name of his derelict slave, he was completely disarmed. Imagine his surprise when he learned that the "scoundrel" had been converted and, even more surprising, had been led to Christ through Paul, the prisoner.

One of the hidden delights of the Christian life is to see God working in marvelous, miraculous ways, revealing Himself in converging circumstances that cannot be explained by coincidence or chance. First Paul had led Philemon to the Lord. Then the apostle had later been arrested and taken to Rome for trial. Philemon's slave had run away and made his way to Rome. Somehow or other he had met Paul and had been converted. The master and the slave were both born again through the same preacher but in widely separated places and under quite different circumstances. Was it a coincidence?

v. 11 The name Onesimus means profitable. But when he ran away, Philemon was probably tempted to call him a worthless rascal. Paul says, in effect, "Yes, he was useless as far as you were concerned, but now he is useful to you and to me." The slave who was returning to Philemon was a better slave than the one who had run away. It has been said that Christian slaves commanded a higher price on the market in New Testament times than others. It should be true today that Christian employees are more valuable as workers than unbelievers.

v. 12 The attitude of the New Testament toward slavery comes into focus in this epistle. We notice that Paul does not condemn slavery or prohibit it. In fact, he sends Onesimus back to his master. But the abuses connected with slavery are condemned and prohibited through the New Testament. "The New Testament . . . meddles directly with no political or social arrangements, but lays down principles which will profoundly affect these, and leaves them to soak into the general mind" (MacLaren). Forcible revolution is never the Bible way to correct social evils. The cause of all man's inhumanity lies in his own fallen nature. The gospel attacks the cause, and offers a new creation in Christ Jesus.

It is conceivable that a slave who has a kind master might be better off than if he were independent. This is true, for instance, of believers, who are bondslaves of the Lord Jesus. Those who are His slaves enjoy the truest form of freedom. In sending Onesimus back to Philemon, Paul was not doing an injustice to the slave. Both master and slave were believers. Philemon would be obligated to treat him with Christian kindness. Onesimus would be expected to serve with Christian faithfulness. The deep affection which the apostle had for Onesimus is expressed in the words "sending my very heart" (A.S.V.). Paul felt as if he were losing a part of himself.

Before leaving this verse, we should notice that the important principle of restitution is set forth. Now that Onesimus was saved, was it necessary for him to return to his former master? The answer is definitely yes. Salvation removes the penalty and power of sin but it does not cancel debts. The new Christian is expected to settle all unpaid accounts and to make right all wrong, insofar as it is humanly possible to do so. Onesimus was obligated to return to his master's service, and to repay any money which he might have stolen.

v. 13 The apostle's personal preference would have been to keep Onesimus with him in Rome. There were many things that the converted slave could have done for Paul while he was imprisoned for the gospel's sake. And this would have been an opportunity for Philemon to minister to the apostle—by providing an assistant. But it would have the drawback of being done without Philemon's knowledge or permission.

v. 14 Paul would not force a kindness from the slave's owner. He would not do anything in connection with Onesimus without Philemon's consent. The kindness would be robbed of its beauty if it were done by compulsion and not by a free and loving willingness.

v. 15 It is a mark of spiritual maturity to be able to look beyond the

173

adverse circumstances of the moment and see God working all things together for good to those who love Him (Romans 8:28). When Onesimus ran away, perhaps Philemon was filled with bitterness and a sense of financial loss. Would he ever see the slave again? Now Paul traces the rainbow through the dark clouds. Onesimus was lost to the family in Colosse for a while that they might have him back for ever. This should be the comfort of Christians who lose believing relatives and friends in death. The separations are for a little while; the reunion will be eternal.

v. 16   Philemon was not only getting Onesimus back—he was receiving him under better conditions than he had ever known him before. It would no longer be the customary master-slave relationship. Onesimus was now better than a slave; he was a brother in the Lord. Henceforth the fear motive would be replaced by the love motive.

Paul had already enjoyed his fellowship as a beloved brother. But now he would no longer have him there in Rome. The apostle's loss would be Philemon's gain. He would now know Onesimus as a brother beloved "both in the flesh and in the Lord" (A.S.V.). The former slave would justify Paul's confidence both "in the flesh," that is, by his devoted service in a physical way, and "in the Lord," that is, by his fellowship as a believer.

v. 17   The apostle's request is startling both in its boldness and in its tenderness. He asks Philemon to receive Onesimus as he would receive the apostle himself. He says, "So if you consider me a partner, receive him as you would receive me" (A.S.V.). The words are reminiscent of the Savior's statements: "He that receiveth you receiveth me and he that receiveth me receiveth him that sent me" (Matthew 10:40), and, "Inasmuch as ye have done it unto one of the least of these my brethren, ye have done it unto me" (Matthew 25:40). They also remind us that God has accepted us in the Person of His Son, that we are as near and dear to God as Christ is.

If Philemon considered Paul as a partner, as one with whom he was in fellowship, then the apostle asks him to receive Onesimus on the same basis. This passage doesn't require that Onesimus be treated as a perpetual guest in the family with no obligation to work. He would still be a servant in the home, but one who belonged to Christ and was therefore a brother in the faith.

The apostle doesn't say that Onesimus had stolen anything from **v. 18** Philemon, but this verse suggests the possibility of such a theft. Certainly theft was one of the cardinal sins of slaves and servants. Paul is willing to accept responsibility for any loss that Philemon might have sustained. He recognizes that restitution should be made. The conversion of Onesimus did not cancel his debts to man. So Paul tells Philemon to charge any loss to his account.

We cannot read this without being reminded of the enormous debt which we had contracted as sinners, and of how it was all charged to the account of the Lord Jesus at Calvary. He paid the debt in full when He died as our Substitute. We are also reminded here of Christ's ministry as our Advocate. When Satan, the accuser of the brethren, brings charges against us for wrongs which we have done, our blessed Lord says in effect, "Charge that to my account." The doctrine of reconciliation is illustrated in this book. Onesimus had been estranged from Philemon because of wrong-doing. Through the ministry of Paul, we have every reason to believe, the distance and "enmity" were removed. The slave was reconciled to his master. So we were estranged from God because of our sin. But through the death and resurrection of Christ, the cause of enmity has been removed and believers are reconciled to God.

Ordinarily the apostle dictated his letter to someone else, writing **v. 19** only the closing verse or two with his own hand. We cannot be sure whether he wrote this entire letter by hand, but at this point at least he took the pen and, in his familiar scrawl, he committed himself to pay any debts incurred by Onesimus. He would do this in spite of the fact that Philemon owed him a considerable debt. Paul had led him to the Lord. He owed his spiritual life to the apostle, as far as the human instrument was concerned. But Paul would not press him for payment of the debt.

Addressing Philemon as "brother," the aged Paul asks only for **v. 20** some benefit in the Lord, some refreshment in Christ. He is pleading that Onesimus be received graciously, that he be forgiven and restored to his place of service in the household—not now as a slave but as a brother in the family of God.

175

CLOSING REMARKS (21-25)

v. 21 The apostle had every confidence that Philemon would do even more than was requested. He himself had been freely forgiven by Christ. He would not do less, surely, for Onesimus. We have here then a vivid illustration of Ephesians 4:32: "And be ye kind one to another, tenderhearted, forgiving one another, even as God for Christ's sake hath forgiven you."

v. 22 But how would Paul know how Philemon had treated Onesimus? He hoped to visit Colosse and to be a guest in Philemon's home. He expected to be released by the civil authorities in answer to the prayers of the Christians. And so he asks Philemon to prepare a guest room for him. Perhaps that would have been one of the first tasks assigned to Onesimus: "Get the guest room ready for our brother, Paul." We do not know whether Paul ever reached Colosse. All we can do is assume that the guest room was ready for him, and that all the members of the household were eager to see him, their hearts having been knitted together in love.

v. 23 Epaphras may have been the one who planted the assembly in Colosse (Colossians 1:7, 8; 4:12, 13). Now a fellow-prisoner with Paul in Rome, he joins in sending greetings to Philemon.

v. 24 With Paul at this time were Mark, Aristarchus, Demas and Luke. These names are also mentioned in Colossians 4:10, 14. Jesus, called Justus, is mentioned in Colossians 4, though omitted here for some reason. *Mark* was the writer of the second Gospel. He had proved to be a faithful servant of the Lord, after his early failure (2 Timothy 4:11, compare Acts 13:13; 15:36-39). *Aristarchus,* a believer from Thessalonica, accompanied Paul on several journeys including the trip to Rome. In Colossians 4:10, Paul called him "my fellow-prisoner." *Demas* later forsook Paul, having loved this present world (2 Timothy 4:10). *Luke,* the beloved physician, proved to be a faithful companion and helper to the end (2 Timothy 4:11).

v. 25 The letter ends with Paul's characteristic benediction. He wishes the grace of Christ to be with Philemon's spirit. Life can hold no greater blessing than the unmerited favor of the Savior as one's moment by moment experience. To walk in the constant realization and enjoyment of His Person and work is all that heart can desire.

Paul laid down his pen and handed the letter to Tychicus for delivery to Philemon. Little did he realize the extent to which the message of this epistle would influence Christian behavior for centuries to follow. The letter is a classic of love and courtesy, as applicable today as it was when it was written.

When you are ready, complete Exam 6 by answering questions 11-20 on pages 181-183. (You should have already answered questions 1-10 as part of your study of lesson 11.)

PHILIPPIANS, COLOSSIANS and PHILEMON

Exam 6
Lessons 11, 12

Exam
Name_____ Grade_____
                (print plainly)

Address _____
                                   Zip   Class
City_____State _____ Code _____ Number _____

Instructor _____

LESSON 11

In the blank space in the right-hand margin write the letter of the correct answer.
(50 points)

1. Philemon was
   a. one of Paul's converts
   b. a centurion in the Roman army
   c. a member of the Philippian church
   d. a runaway slave   _____

2. Onesimus was
   a. a prisoner in Rome
   b. a convert of Paul
   c. a wealthy landowner
   d. a jailor   _____

3. Of all Paul's letters, Philemon is to be regarded as
   a. the most controversial
   b. the most theological
   c. the most personal
   d. the most mystical   _____

4. Paul appealed to Philemon on the ground that he (Paul)
   a. had once done Philemon a favor
   b. was an apostle
   c. was a prisoner
   d. owed his conversion to Philemon's testimony and was there-
      fore "his own son in the faith"   _____

179

5. Philemon lived up to his name. His name means
   a. "lover of God"
   b. "affectionate"
   c. "gentle in spirit"
   d. "guileless"
   _____

6. Archippus is generally thought to have been
   a. the son of Philemon
   b. the brother of Onesimus
   c. the nephew of Paul
   d. the bondslave of Apphia
   _____

7. The house of Philemon was
   a. a meeting place for the assembly of believers in Colosse
   b. a rendezvous for political radicals
   c. a well-known hideout in the underground for runaway slaves
   d. a center of the Gnostic heresy
   _____

8. Paul's greeting of Philemon embodied the desire for Philemon that he might know
   a. faith, hope and love
   b. joy unspeakable and full of glory
   c. grace and peace
   d. the blessing of the Lord which maketh rich and addeth no sorrow thereto
   _____

9. We know that Philemon's faith was productive because we are told that it
   a. produced love toward all the saints
   b. enabled him to overcome sin in his life
   c. moved mountains for God
   d. established a dynamic Christian church at Colosse
   _____

10. We gather from Paul's letter that news of Philemon's overflowing generosity had
   a. come to the ears of the city magistrates at Colosse
   b. brought him under suspicion with the provincial government
   c. reached as far as Rome itself
   d. caused other Christians to become more generous
   _____

LESSON 12

In the blank space in the right-hand margin write the letter of the correct answer.
(50 points)

11. In pleading with Philemon, Paul sought to reach his heart by reminding him that
    a. Onesimus was at his mercy
    b. Paul himself was a prisoner now, and aged
    c. Philemon was himself a freed slave
    d. it was the last favor Paul would ever ask of him since he was to be soon executed _____

12. The placing of the name of Onesimus last implies that
    a. Paul hoped to completely disarm Philemon before ever he reached the name of the runaway slave
    b. as a slave, Onesimus ranked lowest of all in the social scale in the eyes of Paul
    c. Paul was so taken up with memories of Philemon that he almost forgot why he was writing
    d. Paul was really afraid to bring up the subject of Onesimus at all _____

13. The name Onesimus is used as a pun by Paul. The name actually means—
    a, "worthless"
    b. "generous"
    c. "forgiven"
    d. "profitable" _____

14. Paul's attitude towards slavery is revealed in this letter. He
    a. condemned Philemon for owning slaves
    b. urged Philemon to set all his slaves free
    c. ignores the whole question of slavery as too hot to handle
    d. strikes a blow at slavery by stating a principle and allowing time to do the rest _____

15. Paul's feelings for Onesimus were feelings of
    a. sorrow that he must continue as a slave
    b. deep and abiding love
    c. anxiety lest Onesimus be made to suffer for his wrongdoing
    d. relief that at last he would get off his hands this runaway slave who was such a liability to him under prevailing Roman laws regarding the horboring of fugitives _____

16. The new Christian
   a. must make restitution, as far as possible, for wrongs committed in his unconverted days
   b. is forgiven by God and so can ignore his former debts completely
   c. cannot be said to be truly saved until he has made full restitution for his former deeds
   d. can avoid making restitution for former debts so long as he gives generously instead to the work of God _____

17. Paul's personal preference, so far as Onesimus was concerned, would have been to
   a. hand him over to the civil authorities
   b. help him escape both from Rome and from Philemon
   c. send him back to Philemon which, of course, is what he did
   d. keep him with him in Rome because Onesimus had proved himself such a help and encouragement _____

18. Paul requested Philemon to receive Onesimus
   a. with the minimum of displeasure consistent with proper discipline
   b. in accordance with the prescribed legal code for dealing with runaway slaves
   c. in exactly the same way he would receive Paul himself
   d. as he would receive a slave who had been absent on a legitimate errand _____

19. The suggestion has been made that Onesimus had stolen from Philemon. Paul urged Philemon
   a. not to prosecute Onesimus
   b. to make Onesimus repay but not to scourge him for his offense
   c. to see that justice was done
   d. to charge to Paul the full amount owing by Onesimus _____

20. The assembly of which Philemon was a member was probably founded by
   a. Paul
   b. Philemon
   c. Peter
   d. Epaphras
   e. John Mark _____

WHAT DO YOU SAY?

What is your attitude towards those who have wronged you?

_____

_____

_____

_____

_____

BIBLIOGRAPHY

Philippians

Erdman, C. R., *The Epistle of Paul to the Philippians.* Philadelphia: Westminster Press, 1928.

Gifford, E. H., *The Incarnation.* London: Longmans, Green & Co., 1911.

Jowett, J. H., *The High Calling.* London: Andrew Melrose, 1909.

Kelly, Wm., *Lectures on Philippians and Colossians.* London: G. Morrish, No date.

King, Guy, *Joy Way.* London: Marshall, Morgan & Scott, Ltd., 1954.

Meyer, F. B., *Through the Bible Day by Day,* Vol. 7. Philadelphia: American S. S. Union, 1918.

Vine, W. E., *The Epistles to the Philippians and Colossians.* London: Oliphants, 1955.

Williams, George, *The Student's Commentary on the Holy Scriptures.* Grand Rapids: Kregels, 1956.

Bible Versions Used:

The American Standard Version.

Darby, J. N., *The New Testament.* London: G. Morrish, 1904.

Moffatt, James, *The New Testament. A New Translation.* New York: Association Press, 1918.

Way, Arthur S., *The Letters of St. Paul.* Chicago: Moody Press, 1950.

Weymouth, Richard Francis, *The New Testament in Modern Speech.* Boston: The Pilgrim Press, 1943.

In addition to the above, isolated quotations have been made from the writings of C. I. Scofield, Wm. Arnot, T. W. Drury, and A. W. Tozer, but it is no longer possible for the author to document these accurately.

Colossians

English, E. Schuyler, *Studies in the Epistle to the Colossians.* New York: Our Hope Press, 1944.

Erdman, C. R., *Epistles of Paul to the Colossians and Philemon.* Philadelphia: Westminster Press, 1933.

King, Guy, *Crossing the Border*. London: Marshall, Morgan and Scott, Ltd., 1957.

Robertson, A. T., *Paul and the Intellectuals*. Nashville: Sunday School Board of the Southern Baptist Convention, 1928.

Sturz, Richard, *Studies in Colossians*. Chicago: Moody Press, 1955.

Vine, W. E., *The Epistle to the Philippians and Colossians*. London: Oliphants, 1955.

Williams, George, *The Student's Commentary on the Holy Scriptures*. Grand Rapids: Kregels, 1956.

Bible Versions Used:

The American Standard Version

Darby, J. N., *The New Testament*. London: G. Morrish, 1904.

Moffatt, James, *The New Testament. A New Translation*. New York: Association Press, 1918.

Way, Arthur S., *The Letters of St. Paul*. Chicago: Moody Press, 1950.

Weymouth, Richard Francis, *The New Testament in Modern Speech*. Boston: The Pilgrim Press, 1943.